Over All the Mountain Tops

Studies in Austrian Literature, Culture, and Thought

Translation Series

General Editors:

Jorun B. Johns
Richard H. Lawson

Thomas Bernhard

Over All the Mountain Tops

Translated and with an Afterword
by
Michael Mitchell

ARIADNE PRESS
Riverside, California

Ariadne Press would like to express its appreciation to the
Bundeskanzleramt - Sektion Kunst, Vienna for assistance in publishing
this book.

.KUNST

Translated from the German
Über allen Gipfeln ist Ruh
© Suhrkamp Verlag Frankfurt am Main 1981

Library of Congress Cataloging-in-Publication Data

Bernhard, Thomas.
  [Über allen Gipfeln ist Ruh. English]
  Over all the mountain tops / Thomas Bernhard;
  translated and with an afterword by Michael Mitchell.
      p.   cm. -- (Studies in Austrian literature, culture and
  thought. Translation series)
  ISBN 1-57241-128-7
      I. Mitchell, Michael, 1941-   . II. Title. III. Series.
  PT2623.E7U2413 2004
  833'.914--dc22

                                            2004051653

Cover Design:
Art Director: George McGinnis

Over All the Mountain Tops

Over all the mountain tops
Is peace,
In all the tree tops
Not the least
Breath of air:
The birds in the forest are still.
Wait a while, soon you will
Find your peace there.

Goethe

Nietzsche Stieglitz and back do you follow me . . .
Moritz Meister

Dramatis personae

Moritz Meister *author of a tetralogy*
Anne, Frau Meister *his wife*
Fräulein Werdenfels *PhD student, wears spectacles*
Herr von Wegener *Journalist, wears spectacles*
Frau Herta *Home help*
Herr Smirnoff *Mailman*
Meister's Publisher

In the foothills of the Alps
An old villa

SCENE ONE

Outside
Frau Meister and Fräulein Werdenfels (with a camera dangling from her neck)
are setting the table for breakfast

FRAU MEISTER
    My husband Fräulein Werdenfels
    is a stickler for accuracy
    he will not tolerate the least imprecision
    A place for everything and everything in its place
    A pedant Fräulein Werdenfels
    Now that he has completed the tetralogy
    he's full of our journey to Crete again
    In the footsteps of King Minos
    Fräulein Werdenfels steps back and takes a photo of Frau Meister
    The home help doesn't come in the mornings
    I have to do everything myself
    If you haven't seen Crete
    the fountainhead of history so to speak
    My husband sets great store
    by our annual journey
    to sites of ancient culture
    Everything has found its way
    into the tetralogy Fräulein Werdenfels
    Phaestos and Knossos of course
    excavated by Sir Evans
    a man with a bee in his bonnet
    a mad Englishman
    Fräulein Werdenfels takes a photo of the house
    We've studied all the scholarly literature
    We always spend years preparing
    for our cultural journeys
    two years ago in Mexico
    I lost twelve pounds
    She sits down
    You've no idea how much there is to see in the world

and it's open to everyone nowadays
and stands up again
To Crete to the fountainhead
to the source of history
All for the tetralogy
We study what has to be studied
Fräulein Werdenfels takes a photo of Frau Meister
My husband has always
been interested in archaeology
turning to address Fräulein Werdenfels directly
He's more of a scholar than a writer
After all these years even I know
quite a lot about archaeology
I don't want to boast but I've been digging
in Knossos as well
under Sir Wallace Green
exclaims
What joy when your spade strikes a shard
calms down again
The shard upstairs in the library
that magnificent work of art in the early palace style
was dug up by my husband
Fräulein Werdenfels takes a photo of Frau Meister
Have you never been to Knossos

FRÄULEIN WERDENFELS

I'm afraid not

FRAU MEISTER

You really ought to go
that's a gap in your education
especially seeing you come from an academic family
from such a good German family
your father being a professor in Heidelberg

FRÄULEIN WERDENFELS

Yes of course
takes a photo of Frau Meister

FRAU MEISTER

Travel is an education in itself Fräulein Werdenfels

The best people are well traveled
and they prepare themselves well for their travels
not like the masses
Conscientious preparation is *de rigueur*
as my husband always says
A man of culture is never unprepared

suddenly addressing Fräulein Werdenfels directly
Aren't you afraid of catching cold
Fräulein Werdenfels wraps a scarf round her neck
People don't realize how dangerous the winds up here can be
A sensitive person's susceptible once they're over thirty
especially up here among the vineyards
How do you like the area
turns to face the view
isn't it delightful up here
almost completely untouched by these awful modern times
Fräulein Werdenfels steps back and takes a photo of the view
Ideal for a man devoted to things of the mind
Since we moved here my husband has been happy
since he gave up his position as a librarian
Now we're absolutely free
Your lungs feel the benefit too
spreads out a blanket over a bench
Fräulein Werdenfels takes a photo of the view
We're happy here
And one book after another
my husband's really blossomed
Now that the tetralogy's finished
But my husband will tell you about that himself
breathes in deeply
Nothing to disturb us absolutely nothing
adjusts the position of the cups on the table
Everything in its correct placement
People who lack discipline in small things
will lack it in big things too
turning to address Fräulein Werdenfels directly

How long have you been working on your PhD on my
husband
It seems to me it must be incredibly difficult
to come to understand such an *oeuvre*
researching analyzing interpreting
The German is profound
so profound he's afraid says Professor Stieglitz
in the tetralogy
Isn't that superb
Did you know it's quite against his usual principles
for my husband whose life is one of extreme concentration
to allow a PhD student and a female one at that
to spend the night here
When I think how many theses have already
appeared about my husband
It's a signal honor Fräulein Werdenfels
so far the people who visit my husband have always stayed
down
Fräulein Werdenfels takes a photo of the view
in the Golden Dragon
suddenly
Tell me are you related to the General Werdenfels
who instigated that intrigue at the court of the Czar
FRÄULEIN WERDENFELS
My great uncle
FRAU MEISTER
Just as I thought
there's something military about you
something military and aristocratic
my husband will find it very interesting
to hear something about your uncle the field marshal
my husband's a genealogist as well
and he's always been fascinated by the high-ranking military
Fräulein Werdenfels takes a photo of Frau Meister
I'm not photogenic at all Fräulein Werdenfels
She tidies her hair and Fräulein Werdenfels takes another photo of her
Originally my husband wanted to be a soldier

a field marshal of course
sits down
It's really lovely up here isn't it
Away from the city and all the disturbance
We don't pay anything no rent
The city's happy
to have a famous man like my husband here
We show our gratitude of course
we give to the poor the simple folk
Months before Christmas I'm knitting bed-jackets
for the old people in the old folks' home
and every year my husband writes a Christmas poem
and it's read out in City Hall on Christmas Eve
always by a famous actor
last year Herr Quadflieg the famous Faust
read it
Quadflieg's one of our friends of course
sits up and points out something in the distance
Look Fräulein Werdenfels there
that's where my husband comes from
Fräulein Werdenfels take a few steps forward
Frau Meister stands up
You can see his parents' house
There If you look between those two birch trees
behind the abandoned brickworks
Fräulein Werdenfels takes a photo of the distant view
You see those sheep in the foreground
in the background's my husband's parents' house
From slater's apprentice to famous author
Fräulein Werdenfels takes a photo of the distant view
That's where he came from Fräulein Werdenfels just imagine
from nothing from less than nothing
turning to face Fräulein Werdenfels directly
I hope you slept well Fräulein Werdenfels
or did the goats down in the valley wake you up
FRÄULEIN WERDENFELS
No I slept wonderfully well

FRAU MEISTER

> At night up here you hear nothing but the rustle of the vine leaves
> There's always a gentle breeze from the west Fräulein Werdenfels
> from the west here
> *Both sit down*
> *turning to address Fräulein Werdenfels directly*
> Just imagine the city council's decided
> to name a street after my husband
> Moritz-Meister-Straße
> Who would have thought it
> It makes all the effort worthwhile
> And my husband has been elected a member
> of the Academy of Language and Literature

FRÄULEIN WERDENFELS

> Oh

FRAU MEISTER

> Yes you heard correctly
> Now my husband's an academician as well
> he won't admit it
> but he's really proud of being elected
> Unanimously Fräulein Werdenfels unanimously
> And the President was elected at the same time as my husband
> incredible isn't it
> such an eminent statesman
> and such a great important author at the same time
> There'll be a big celebration in Darmstadt
> *stands up, Fräulein Werdenfels starts to stand up too*
> Oh don't get up
> *takes a few steps and breathes in deeply, Fräulein Werdenfels stays seated*
> Suddenly the moment he deserves has come after all
> suddenly raised to the heights
> What joy
> *turns round to face the table, Fräulein Werdenfels stands up*
> Of course there are jealous tongues
> but there always are

You really are pretty
hard to believe you're such a scholar
My husband is most complimentary about you
such an intelligent young person he said to me
attentive and receptive all evening
such an attentive young lady all evening
He says you've read every sentence he's written
not only read
but you can quote them at a moment's notice
I really admire people like that
I can't remember a thing
it drives my husband to distraction sometimes
looks at Fräulein Werdenfels's necklace
A beautiful piece
precious
a family heirloom I'm sure

FRÄULEIN WERDENFELS

Yes from my grandmother
it came from the queen of Montenegro

FRAU MEISTER

Isn't genuine old jewelery lovely
I've wanted an amber necklace for a long time
one particular amber necklace
well when he gets the prize
whispers something to Fräulein Werdenfels

FRÄULEIN WERDENFELS *exclaims*

The Wilhelm Raabe Prize
oh how wonderful

FRAU MEISTER

I've thought for a long time
really
my husband ought to get the Raabe Prize
having been a librarian in Brunswick
Now it's happened
But he doesn't know yet
I haven't told him yet
The burgomaster of Brunswick passed on the news to me

turns towards the vineyard, stands on tiptoe and calls out
Moritz Moritz
Mooooritz
to Fräulein Werdenfels
If he didn't have his bees
He's mad about bees
Mad about insects
but mad about bees above all
He lives and breathes for his bees alone
he often spends the whole day in his bee-house
Bees and literature
turns towards the vineyard again and calls out
Moritz Moritz
breakfast
to Fräulein Werdenfels
His whole life revolves round his bees
he's written a study
a study that reveals the secret of the bees
The Bee as a Work of Art the study's called
But do sit down Fräulein Werdenfels
Fräulein Werdenfels does not sit down but looks across at the vineyard
with Frau Meister
When we came here
my husband said
now I can write again
and he started writing book after book
oh I'm so happy the tetralogy's
finished at last
it was the most difficult task
he set himself
Fräulein Werdenfels takes a photo of the view
three whole years he spent writing it
or twenty years strictly speaking
I had to read to him from it every day
he said he had to *hear* what he'd written
to be able to form a judgment
every day four to eight pages

above all the chapters concerning Professor Stieglitz
depending on how he felt
Fräulein Werdenfels takes a photo of the view
It's not easy for me either Fräulein Werdenfels
with a man such as my husband
who demands only the best
He didn't make any more changes
he drew Professor Stieglitz
like himself
completely autobiographical
no previous book flowed from his pen
so perfect onto the page Fräulein Werdenfels
You know my husband writes everything
by hand
in the classic manner
my husband hates the typewriter
The tetralogy ends with the union of the brothers and sisters
that wonderful ending on the Acropolis
my husband is a master at endings
Edgar comes back from New York
and meets Robert in Constantinople
and then Lynn and Susanne come from Poland
and they all celebrate their return
as a storm looms on the horizon
How calmly Moritz brings it to its conclusion
In the house of Zarkis the art dealer Robert sits down
at the piano and plays Chopin
and Professor Stieglitz deciphers their story, a story that is
history
the history of ideas Fräulein Werdenfels
and they all listen and are reconciled
a truly German book Moritz says
there's been nothing like it since Thomas Mann
such unity of structure
and in such serenely flowing language
corresponding perfectly to the content of the tetralogy
Of course as my husband says this is

a book for the more discerning among us
the educated reader will derive much profit from it
especially the central Stieglitz chapter
I'm full of admiration for the way Moritz has done it
He gets up at three in the morning wraps himself in the horse-
blanket
he brought back from Sicily twenty years ago
sits down at his desk and writes until nine
like Professor Stieglitz in the tetralogy
then washes and dresses and goes to see his bees
Fräulein Werdenfels takes a photo of the view
we take breakfast at ten
like Professor Stieglitz in the tetralogy
of course it all depends on the bees
We're very happy up here Fräulein Werdenfels

SCENE TWO

As in the previous scene
A large sunshade
Frau Meister and Fräulein Werdenfels on a bench
FRAU MEISTER
In the afternoon
I often sit here for hours Fräulein Werdenfels
and think to myself
just to myself
my husband's working
Then I hear him get up
and walk up and down his room twice
Then it's time
for me to make his supper
When he's working he can only take light food
the very lightest
While he was writing the tetralogy
I couldn't even give him the ham he likes so much
a bowl of yogurt that was all

You know Fräulein Werdenfels
my happiest moments
are when I can say now he's finished
Fräulein Werdenfels stands up, steps backward, takes a photo of Frau
Meister and sits down again
the manuscript's finished
and he puts it aside for a week or two
doesn't even touch it again
then we wrap it up
and send it off to the publisher
Of course you'll meet my husband's publisher
this evening
We are really fortunate that my husband
found this publisher
who as you know has only published the greatest
and most important authors
always the best of the German writers
and the most famous from France and England
From the very beginning my husband appeared
among the very greatest minds
along with the most outstanding names
I don't need to tell you them all
But for a long time my husband was overshadowed
he was always the genius he is today
but overshadowed
like Professor Stieglitz in the tetralogy
Fräulein Werdenfels gets up and takes a photo
the world was simply blind to his genius
which had created masterpieces of the greatest significance
But it's probably the same as my husband says about Professor
Stieglitz
that genius develops better unknown and out of the limelight
than in the public eye
where it's very soon burnt out, finished
My husband says late recognition has something tremendous
about it
Fräulein Werdenfels takes another photo and sits down again

When it's suddenly there
illuminating a complete *oeuvre*
so that all at once it's clearly visible to all
The most important novelist of the second half of the century
as the *Süddeutsche Zeitung* wrote
a paper that ignored my husband for forty years
Things that blossom late will last
very often forever so my husband says
It's something special you know
when the president of the Academy of Language and Literature
comes here in person
and when the Federal President sends a telegram of
congratulation
twenty-two words not counting the address
Did you read the article my husband wrote in the *Neue
Rundschau*
He spent three days in Knossos
silent and alone
like Professor Stieglitz in the tetralogy
then sat down at his desk in the hotel in Herakleion
where we were staying
and wrote his study of King Minos
like Professor Stieglitz
What a loss to archaeology
My husband gets his best ideas when he's with his bees
with his bees and at breakfast
like Professor Stieglitz in the tetralogy
he'll suddenly jump up and run into the house
to write something down
A brief note that may be completely unrelated
at least that's how it seems
will lead him to an important philosophical idea
And how many poems owe their origin to something
that occurred to him over breakfast
The poem about the crested lark for example
I'd just asked him if he wanted me to comb his hair
after he had eaten his egg

his rheumatism was acting up again
when he suddenly leaped up
and ran into the house and came back soon after
with the poem he titled "The Crested Lark"
Listen
recites
In this busy world of fear
The lark sought peace and respite here
Unfortunately I can't remember any more
Fräulein Werdenfels writes something down in her notebook
He dedicated it to the president of the Academy of Language
and Literature
Recently he's started writing poetry again
The poems you see are starting to flow again
after all the philosophy
suddenly the poems are coming again
I've got time for poetry again he says
looks around
We live in such modest circumstances here
such a simple life
like Professor Stieglitz in the tetralogy
It's essential for my husband
He has always hated possessions
like Stieglitz
People are suffocated by their possessions he says
Fräulein Werdenfels notes something down
Possessions make people ill
my husband says in the tetralogy
over the years they crush them
The thinking man must be free of possessions
In this busy world of fear
The lark sought peace and respite here
He always finds the right rhyme
don't you agree
FRÄULEIN WERDENFELS
    Yes always the right rhyme
    that's something I've always admired about his sonnets

that he always found the right rhyme
FRAU MEISTER
My husband doesn't cheat
a rhyme must be a proper rhyme he says
Fräulein Werdenfels makes a note
His sonnets have been reissued
a beautiful book
he wrote it for young people he speaks to their hearts
leans back, pauses then suddenly exclaims
Bellini of course Bellini
All the time I've been trying to think
who wrote *Norma*
of course it's Bellini
I heard Callas at La Scala in Milan
But I didn't think her voice was all that exceptional
always a little husky
perhaps even slightly vulgar don't you think
FRÄULEIN WERDENFELS
Yes perhaps
FRAU MEISTER
We'd gone to Milan for supper
and being in Milan
of course
we went to the opera where they were doing *Norma*
I'm not all that keen on Italian opera
my husband's an enthusiast
a great admirer of Verdi
for him there is nothing to beat *La Traviata*
The cultured German with a passion for Italian opera
You should see my husband
he abandons himself to the music completely
But of course that all comes from the fact that
originally my husband wanted to be a singer
but it's a wish that was not to be fulfilled
Every exceptional artist
bears in his heart a secret wish
that has not been fulfilled

his heartfelt wish
Fräulein Werdenfels makes a note
You can tell from every line my husband writes
that he's a highly musical person
and a sensitive reader will also see
that my husband wanted to be a singer
like Professor Stieglitz
He would have been a brilliant *lieder* singer
The *Winterreise* sung by him
that would be the ultimate
but it wasn't to be
Suddenly his voice was gone you see
it's terrible for an artist
when his instrument suddenly fails him
the instrument that is his life
Fräulein Werdenfels makes a note
My husband has a quite different approach
to the interpretation of *lieder* than is the fashion today
As far a *lieder* are concerned
he's a romantic
A pity you've never heard him sing
it would explain much in his literary *oeuvre*
You really need to read what he has written
and at the same time hear his voice
but of course that's not possible
It means his writing is never truly understood
that's how he sees it himself
Fräulein Werdenfels makes a note
My husband always finds it relaxing
after a large-scale prose work
to turn to the short, the lighter form of the lyric
and then sometimes
he might decide to produce an essay
a short piece of polished scientific prose
something about bees or the origins of rocks
It's such a pity these little jewels
have not been published

but the time will come when they too will be published
says Professor Stieglitz in the tetralogy
little masterpieces Fräulein Werdenfels
that bear comparison with Goethe's great works on natural
history
My husband is often completely worn out
when he's finished a large-scale work of fiction
He is of course a writer of fiction first and foremost
although he is a master of every form of literature
like Stieglitz in the tetralogy
but first and foremost a writer of prose fiction
which he sees as the modern epic
Poetry prose philosophy the philosophy of natural history
never the dramatic form
the fact is my husband hates drama
he calls it a cheap vulgar art
like Professor Sieglitz in the tetralogy
Fräulein Werdenfels makes a note
Of course when people talk about him
it's Meister the writer of prose fiction they're talking about
but there's still a poet inside him
the poetry still comes welling up Fräulein Werdenfels
I'm accompanying my husband on his reading tour
He doesn't know yet
he's going to do this reading tour
but I've already signed all the contracts
From Flensburg to Berchtesgaden
forty-seven towns
from the North Sea to the Alps
my husband will be reading extracts from his tetralogy
He's his own best interpreter
He'll read tonight
if we're lucky
a private performance
for the select few so to speak
probably even
something from the tetralogy

his publisher's very keen to hear it you know
We'll have a fire
and sit round it to listen to him
my husband doesn't like reading from his work and that's the
truth
but I'll persuade him
I've always managed to persuade him
once the flames are crackling in the hearth
he won't be able to refuse
You have to give men a quiet push
to get them to do what has to be done
He's to read the conclusion
the end
where Professor Stieglitz suddenly comes in
where everything resolves itself in perfect harmony
His publisher will say
he wants to take the manuscript with him
but I won't let him have it
we're keeping it here for a while I'll say
we're not letting go of it just yet
keep the publisher on tenterhooks for a while longer
In this busy world of fear
The lark sought peace and respite here
A vision in the meadow green
Of primal nature pure serene
You see you just have to wait
and it comes back to you
A vision in the meadow green
Of primal nature pure serene
that's how the third and fourth lines go
Fräulein Werdenfels makes a note
Herr Meister comes from the bee-house with a veil over his head
About time too Moritz
Fräulein Werdenfels jumps up and takes a photo of Herr Meister
Fräulein Werdenfels and I have been waiting for ages
didn't you hear me calling
Nothing can distract you once you're with your beloved bees

Fräulein Werdenfels takes another photo of Herr Meister
HERR MEISTER *tries to take off the veil but can't manage it*
Take the veil off for me please
Frau Meister takes the veil off over his head
Goethe didn't understand bees
I've discovered that today
Everything he wrote about bees is wrong
Such a great mind as Goethe
and everything wrong
hands back the veil to his wife who had given it to him
We always think
everything in and about a great mind must be right
but we are mistaken
Now I have the proof
that Goethe was mistaken as far as bees are concerned
FRAU MEISTER
But what does it matter
Fräulein Werdenfels laughs
HERR MEISTER
You're right
what does it matter
shakes hands with Fräulein Werdenfels
Fräulein Werdenfels curtsies
We study life
go deeper and deeper
and the darkness gets greater and greater
Is that not so Fräulein Werdenfels
takes off his green apron and hands it to his wife
Research that is what we are all doing
research Fräulein Werdenfels research
to Frau Meister, after having scrutinized the breakfast table
Everything as it should be on the breakfast table
only where is *The Elective Affinities*
Frau Meister dashes into the house
Our reading our breakfast reading
Before we drink our fruit juice
we read a few pages

that's the way we do things out here among the vineyards
a philosophical text of course
our breakfast isn't complete
without a reading from a philosophical text
or at least a literary text of a philosophical nature
takes Fräulein Werdenfels by the arm and inhales deeply
Ever since we have been together
we have kept company with the great minds
my wife and I
otherwise we wouldn't have been able to survive Fräulein
Werdenfels
Frau Meister returns with The Elective Affinities
The Elective Affinities
what a magnificent book
Fräulein Werdenfels steps back and takes a photo of Herr and Frau
Meister
Goethe is our guiding spirit
as Professor Stieglitz says in my tetralogy
But now let us proceed to breakfast
Fräulein Werdenfels
takes her arm and they all go to sit down

SCENE THREE

As in the previous scene
Herr and Frau Meister and Fräulein Werdenfels are having breakfast
You know Fräulein Werdenfels
it was my heartfelt wish
to be a singer
to stand on the stage
as a central figure in a great opera
Othello Fräulein Werdenfels Iago
But a little cold a sore throat
I caught on Ischia strangely enough
destroyed my dream
To see what might be a brilliant career ahead of you

then suddenly no prospects at all as an artist
FRAU MEISTER
> And that happened to my husband
> who is a more musical person than anyone else I know
> He has all of Beethoven's great symphonies in his head
> like Professor Stieglitz in the tetralogy
> Even as a child he was highly gifted musically
> not just a pastime Fräulein Werdenfels
HERR MEISTER
> Now you mustn't exaggerate Anne
> but even Mendelssohn I can hear complete with every part
> when I'm lying on my sofa for example
> and need one particular mood of my sensibility
> I hear Mendelssohn
> a composer of the second rank in absolute terms even if first-class
FRAU MEISTER
> Do have some honey Fräulein Werdenfels
> it's from my husband's bee-house
> from our bees Fräulein Werdenfels
HERR MEISTER
> Or Rachmaninov for example
> When I was very young
> I had a friend who wanted to be a pianist
> It was from her I first heard Rachmaninov
> in fact all the more important Russian composers
> So highly gifted musically
> she opened up the world of music for me like a casket
> impossible to say how much I owe that young woman
> she died suddenly no one knew what of
> a highly musical person like that
> takes all that exceptional knowledge to the grave with her
> that immense musicality
> such as I have never come across since
> When I was young I always thought
> I'd be what one might call an interpretative artist
> a musician

I loved the double bass above all
FRAU MEISTER
Like Professor Stieglitz
HERR MEISTER
I had not the slightest affinity with the piano
that's absurd isn't it Fräulein Werdenfels
My wife is a piano virtuoso
a soloist of the highest order
she gave solo concerts herself in her earlier days
Once she even played under Furtwängler in the Konzerthaus in
Vienna
then suddenly it was all over
just imagine
after we married
my wife gave no more concerts
only one of us can dedicate his life to Art we decided
The choice fell on me
but of course my wife plays the piano every day
so as not to get out of practice
turning to address his wife directly
I'm sure you'll hear her this afternoon
You'll give us a little sample of your playing won't you
That is a true sacrifice
to deny oneself for another for the one you share your life with
My wife had made a name for herself
and gave up everything
at the peak of success
all that traveling
all the applause from the crowd
But what is true is that her playing has reached
a greater degree of perfection than before
turning to address his wife directly
away from the crowds you have developed complete mastery
over your instrument
and I alone am here to witness it I alone
As for me it turned out
that I am not an interpretative but a creative artist

FRAU MEISTER

The writer inside my husband suddenly came to life
I'm sure it must be of the greatest importance for your thesis
to learn precisely how my husband developed
Don't be afraid to grill my husband Fräulein Werdenfels
You'll be on the trail of Professor Stieglitz

HERR MEISTER

In Regensburg I remember it precisely
I had gone with my uncle a steward for the Thurn und Taxis
estates
to the cathedral there
a masterpiece of German Gothic art by the way Fräulein
Werdenfels
Your education isn't complete
if you haven't seen it
write it down Regensburg
Würzburg and Regensburg
but above all Regensburg
It was in Regensburg Cathedral that it suddenly became clear to
me
underneath the net vaulting
underneath a tiny opening in the net vaulting
it became clear to me that I was destined to be a writer

FRAU MEISTER

Like Professor Stieglitz

HERR MEISTER

Will you pass me another roll Anne
Frau Meister gives him a roll
There was nothing to suggest it beforehand
even if like all German boys of course
when I was still a schoolboy at the classical high school
I wrote verses
some of which are still fixed in my mind and in my heart
yes they are
even though they couldn't have been perfect yet
a lot has been lost from that period
for example a sonnet cycle on yarrow

FRAU MEISTER
    Like Professor Stieglitz
HERR MEISTER
    But I think it's better that way
    Then these scholars come along from Heidelberg
    and from Marburg an der Lahn
    with the ink on their degree certificates hardly dry
    tracking down literature
    dragging everything out into the open
    in their overeagerness
    No no Fräulein Werdenfels
    all these early creations must remain a sealed book to posterity
    even if they're not completely lost
    they are a sealed book for literary studies
    That is not to say
    that I am ashamed of my early works on the contrary
    Stieglitz in the tetralogy wasn't ashamed either
    everything an artist has produced is part of his *oeuvre*
FRÄULEIN WERDENFELS
    You put that beautifully
HERR MEISTER
    Many of my fellow writers are ashamed of their early work
    and do everything to try and conceal it
    I am not like that no indeed not
    Every young person is gifted and writes verse
    Sometimes when in remarkably cheerful mood Goethe used to
    say
    says Stieglitz
    I only have to look at these early works
    poems short stories prose
    and it puts me in a quite melancholy mood
    But of course I have no intention of releasing them
    when my mature works form such a unified whole
    that would be irresponsible wouldn't it Fräulein Werdenfels
FRÄULEIN WERDENFELS
    But one day Professor Meister
    posterity will makes these works publicly available too

You have no right to keep these treasures under lock and key
in my opinion
one day
HERR MEISTER
Yes perhaps perhaps that's true perhaps you're right
I wrote whole cycles on the Morello cherry for example
when I was fifteen
But Stieglitz expresses all this precisely
It must have all been there inside me from the start
Stieglitz says in the tetralogy
Of course my parents were not entirely sympathetic
to my artistic leanings
addresses his wife directly
nor were yours to yours either
FRAU MEISTER
My parents didn't object to my studying music
but they certainly weren't enthusiastic about it
HERR MEISTER
I come from a family with no interest in the arts
I'm from a very modest background
like Professor Stieglitz
my father was a very minor clerk in a large brickworks
I couldn't expect him to understand
and my mother was the daughter of a laborer
It's easy to say that now
but it is the truth the bitter truth Fräulein Werdenfels
You yourself come from an academic family
a family of scholars
an immeasurably rich breeding ground for art and science
From fairly affluent circumstances too
while I
points into the distance
Over there do you see where it's rather barren
that's where I was born
two cows and four acres that was all
and despised by the locals as well

FRAU MEISTER
>But it's all turned out well Moritz
>you've made it
>we have what we need
>and you're famous a famous man

FRÄULEIN WERDENFELS
>Our revered author
>our world-famous author even
>about whom as many books will soon have appeared
>as he has written himself

FRAU MEISTER
>A book on my husband has appeared in Paris
>published by Gallimard

HERR MEISTER
>A study of my style
>very interesting

FRAU MEISTER
>I'm sure you speak excellent French
>don't you Fräulein Werdenfels
>you read French

HERR MEISTER
>Well of course she does
>with a background like that

FRÄULEIN WERDENFELS
>I hadn't heard of that book

HERR MEISTER
>It only came out two weeks ago

FRAU MEISTER
>Beautifully produced
>like all Gallimard's wonderful books
>Unfortunately my French is rather poor

HERR MEISTER
>My wife is too modest
>of course she speaks French
>better even than Italian of which, as a virtuoso musician,
>she has an excellent understanding
>as Stieglitz says at a crucial point

FRAU MEISTER

> Until he was twenty-two my husband wrote only poems
> then nothing at all for several years
> he wanted to pursue his career as a singer
> then at thirty-two his first prose piece
> a short piece entitled The Lily
> it was even published

HERR MEISTER

> in the All-Saints-Day number of the *Stuttgarter Zeitung*
> I can't remember the precise date
> but it had a whole page to itself
> I was very proud of myself
> and although it was very cold
> I sat on a bench in the park opposite the theater
> the paper open at my piece on my lap
> and thought
> that all the passers-by would know
> that The Lily printed in the paper that day
> was by me
> Stieglitz gives a precise account
> So overnight I had become an author
> a feature in the German literary landscape
> of course at that time I had a very romantic idea of literature
> but from then on I wrote regularly
> And there was one more poem
> about a birch tree gently swaying in the evening breeze
> The birth of a writer is a lengthy process with many painful
> setbacks

FRÄULEIN WERDENFELS

> You put that very beautifully Professor

FRAU MEISTER

> Until finally the great writer's there
> until the universally revered writer emerges
> from his trials and travails
> as Stieglitz puts it

HERR MEISTER

> In one of my late poems

in the collection The End of the Moth by the way
that I published with Klett
the birch tree gently swaying in the evening breeze reappears
in a quite different context of course
as a religious element with philosophical connotations
FRAU MEISTER
You wrote it in Nuremberg
during the Catholic Conference
we'd been invited by Cardinal Frings
we were sitting next to Frings
pointing out the positions
Frings was sitting there and I was sitting next to Frings and my
husband was sitting
here next to me
And my husband read from The End of the Moth
My husband is a great admirer of Dürer
HERR MEISTER
Like my Professor Stieglitz as it happens
FRAU MEISTER
He loves half-timbered houses
And secretly *The Mastersingers* is your favorite opera
isn't it Moritz
or am I giving away a secret there
After all Fräulein Werdenfels needs to know about
your categorical likes and dislikes in the arts
HERR MEISTER
Wagner makes one's heart beat faster
Stieglitz says in the tetralogy
Nietzsche and Wagner it's all very interesting isn't it
One's priorities are important
priorities are what matter
FRAU MEISTER
What's that poem called
you wrote during the Catholic Conference in Nuremberg
HERR MEISTER
Dürer in Fürth

FRAU MEISTER
    Of course Dürer in Fürth
    My husband loves vowels
    it's important to know that
    Stieglitz loves vowels too
HERR MEISTER
    I was looking out of the hotel window
FRAU MEISTER
    The White Raven
HERR MEISTER
    Precisely
    and saw a birch tree like the birch tree
    outside my parents' house
    it inspired me
    less than five minutes and the poem was there
    The artist never knows
    how his creation came to be
    all he is left with is conjecture
    the true artist knows nothing of his art
    only gradually does he come to understand
    what ultimately still remains hidden from him
    In the evening I read the poem
    in a select group
    to Cardinal Frings
    Then it was included in the Catholic reader for schools in
    North Rhine-Westphalia
    I didn't accept a fee of course
    turning to address Fräulein Werdenfels directly
    And just imagine
    on Christmas Eve nineteen hundred and sixty-eight
    the birch tree outside my parents' house
    Professor Stieglitz loves the birch tree too you know
    that birch tree that turned into a poem
    was sawn down
    by my parents' neighbors
    my parents were still alive
    because of some disagreement about a piece of land

just imagine brutally sawn down
out of hatred
FRAU MEISTER
It went to court
the proceedings lasted three whole years
My parents-in-law lost the case
The judge took the view
that the birch tree cast too much shade on the neighboring
property
A most unpleasant affair
addresses her husband directly
wasn't it
HERR MEISTER
People show no consideration for others
hatred between neighbors is the worst
FRAU MEISTER
My husband was a real opera fanatic
I found that attractive of course
since I was and still am a musician myself
I couldn't have married an unmusical man
HERR MEISTER
Mad about opera like my Professor Stieglitz
FRAU MEISTER
The more dramatic the better
HERR MEISTER
My father hated opera
FRAU MEISTER
That's what made my husband into an opera fanatic
The bell rings at the garden gate
She jumps up
The mailman
She runs to the garden gate and comes back with the Mailman who is
carrying a heavy bag
Do come in come in Herr Smirnoff
we're just having breakfast
we have a charming visitor
they come to the table

HERR MEISTER

What nice things have you got for us today Herr Smirnoff
The Mailman empties his bag out on a chair

FRAU MEISTER

Unbelievable how much mail there is

HERR MEISTER

Unbelievable
Just see how much mail we get
Fräulein Werdenfels

FRAU MEISTER

And that almost every day
isn't that so Herr Smirnoff

HERR MEISTER

Since I achieved a modicum of fame

FRAU MEISTER

That's enough false modesty
why don't you just admit you enjoy it
goes through the letters on the chair, then
Nothing but requests from the universities
for my husband to give a reading
picks up two letters
From the University of Nancy
And from the German Academy for Language and Literature

HERR MEISTER

Come and join us Herr Smirnoff

FRAU MEISTER

Do sit down Herr Smirnoff

FRÄULEIN WERDENFELS

An interesting name
for a mailman

FRAU MEISTER

Herr Smirnoff's parents were Bulgarian
he reminds my husband a bit of Chaliapin
don't you agree
his general appearance
What a land of song Bulgaria

*offers the Mailman a seat beside Fräulein Werdenfels and he has to sit
down*
The war scattered mankind to the four winds
and that's how Herr Smirnoff came to Germany
as a very small child
But you feel you're completely German don't you Herr
Smirnoff
MAILMAN
Oh yes
Fräulein Werdenfels gets up to take a photo
FRAU MEISTER
The very image of Chaliapin
What a singer
revolutionized opera
The singer my husband admired above all
*pours tea for the Mailman, gives him a roll and they all move closer
together for a photo*
You came just at the right moment Herr Smirnoff
Fräulein Werdenfels takes a step backwards and takes the photo
His parents were gardeners
Bulgarians always are
Fräulein Werdenfels sits back down
And how are your children Herr Smirnoff
no problems at school I should imagine
HERR MEISTER
Gifted children very gifted children
FRAU MEISTER
German children really completely German
they all have German names
Herr Smirnoff is married to a German woman
You have a nice wife Herr Smirnoff
looks through the mail and takes out a few more letters
Lots of books people want him to sign
My husband does that after lunch
he doesn't like doing it but he does it
You mustn't disappoint loyal readers
What is a writer without readers

He's nothing without readers
to the Mailman
Where would you be without the mail Herr Smirnoff
You without the mail Herr Smirnoff
they all laugh
A letter from the Bavarian State Chancellery
and a letter from the mayor's office in Zurich
and a letter from Stockholm
goes over to her husband and holds the letter in front of his face
From Stockholm
from Stockholm
from Stockholm

SCENE FOUR

The library
Herr Meister in a rocking chair, Fräulein Werdenfels sitting opposite him
with her camera and her notebook, in which she is making notes
HERR MEISTER *smoking a pipe*
Ask your questions Fräulein Werdenfels
just go ahead and ask
The experience of war
is the fundamental experience of the German male
Odessa Minsk Sebastopol
finally the Western Front Normandy
When you've seen your comrades as I have
Fräulein Werdenfels gets up to take a photo
frozen stiff mutilated
Of course a writer digests and utilizes
everything he has experienced
the whole of his past history that has gone to form him
every writer every literary artist is the product
of the whole of past history
Of course it is a privileged state being a writer
in which death plays a quite exceptional role
perhaps the experience of death is paramount

Fräulein Werdenfels kneels down and takes the photo
Death the experience of death that means maturity
look at all these young writers
so very gifted young people all of them
they write so fluently
they write so much today
Fräulein Werdenfels sits down again
but they have no experience behind them
the things they write fall apart as you read them
they are nothing because they lack a sense of history
as Professor Stieglitz says
because they lack the experience of death
because they lack the confrontation with death
because the foundation is not cannot be there
The writer must have everything firmly anchored within him
the origins of mankind the origins of culture
as I said the whole of history as Stieglitz says
FRÄULEIN WERDENFELS
What gave you the idea for the tetralogy
and when did the idea of the tetralogy first appear
HERR MEISTER
The idea of the tetralogy
indubitably my magnum opus
so far at least
had always been there in my head
The figure of Stieglitz first of all of course
I can't say at this or that particular point
that exciting idea was suddenly there
and from that moment on I pursued it passionately obsessively
The idea is there demanding to be pursued
it towers up before one higher and higher
as if one had an immense mountain range to climb
if one loses heart it will be impossible
to lose heart would bring everything to naught
before one had even started
FRÄULEIN WERDENFELS
Such a large-scale work

a work of two thousand pages
encompassing the whole of cultural history
how is that possible
HERR MEISTER
It is impossible to say
absolutely impossible to say
A philosopher cannot say he is philosophizing
a writer cannot say he is writing
a creator cannot say he is creating
my Professor Stieglitz says in the tetralogy
The endless pains
which one must take with every line
Stieglitz says
It is something one simply cannot imagine
Failure is there in every work of art
but with the grace of God we can succeed
we work our way in as into a mine
dig deeper and deeper bring our finds to the surface
Stieglitz says
FRÄULEIN WERDENFELS
Did you have a plan for the tetralogy
HERR MEISTER
Of course I had a plan
the whole concept was there
in the basic idea
the idea of Stieglitz you understand
a plan worked out in detail in my head
Professor Stieglitz the German as pure mind
but then when I set about it and go down into the mine
I am immersed in icy darkness
as Stieglitz says
FRÄULEIN WERDENFELS
You have woven so much of the history of the human mind
into this tetralogy
HERR MEISTER
Well yes you see first of all the endless task
the thousands of books one has to have studied

just to tackle such a theme
the theme of how we became human
if I may put it like that
if I may quote my Professor Stieglitz
everything is against one at the start says Stieglitz
everything
as I said the image of an immense mountain range
in the truest sense of the word
And the certainty of the possibility
of failure at any moment
For nothing is certain nothing
One is working at a lifelong task
and one has nothing to show for it
nothing is guaranteed
for the artist the writer
Stieglitz says to himself in the Dolomites
Then one finally reaches the point where one can start
where one can start to write
then one gets some ridiculous indisposition
a little tummy upset blood poisoning
and one is back at square one
countless new starts again and again
it demands the tenacity of a beast of prey
to quote Stieglitz word for word
rocks to and fro a few times
The catastrophe is being completely on one's own of course
being truly left to one's own devices
Nietzsche Stieglitz and back do you follow me
Nobody no one nothing can help one
It is a fight one must take up on one's own
my Sils Maria as Stieglitz confesses
reliant on one's own resources
and it is a fight
the writer is fighting for his life
that's how my Professor Stieglitz puts it
FRÄULEIN WERDENFELS
    What kind of characters are there in your tetralogy

HERR MEISTER

> Different characters highly dissimilar
> different minds as you would expect
> My aim was to portray all possible contrary characters
> the whole spectrum so to speak of humankind
> Robert the scientist for example
> who comes to grief must come to grief
> through his science
> or Irma the failure who gave up in Paris
> probably at the wrong moment
> because she did not understand Stieglitz
> The whole spectrum as I said the whole spectrum
> all of them characters such as you will find today
> after all it's a book of our time not of any other time
> Stieglitz says at a crucial point
> not possible at any other
> as Stieglitz says exhausted mentally exhausted in St. Moritz
> it is not a book of any time you like
> it is the book of our time
> as Stieglitz says

FRÄULEIN WERDENFELS

> Is not Robert something like
> the negative hero in your tetralogy

HERR MEISTER

> You could put it like that Fräulein Werdenfels
> but then on the other hand it's not the case
> just think What is the negative hero
> It's the hero full stop
> a human being who has failed
> as Professor Stieglitz says
> the failed failure so to speak

FRÄULEIN WERDENFELS

> The failure left behind by history
> who fails to make his mark on history

HERR MEISTER

> The failure who fails *the test of* history
> the failure who fails *himself* in failing to face up to history

But of course it was by no means my intention
to portray what you call the negative hero alone
no what I wanted to reveal
through the individual characters
is that there is no escaping history
In Edgar for example I created someone entirely characteristic
of our times
who never comes to terms with life
cannot come to terms with life
although his is a mind with everything at its fingertips
in fact it is precisely for that reason Edgar fails
He is the great artist
he is the great mathematician
he is the eminent scientist
he is the universal mind
and fails
as my Professor Stieglitz says
I sketched it very elegantly
perhaps a touch too elegantly perhaps
FRÄULEIN WERDENFELS
Did you have problems with style in the Edgar chapter
HERR MEISTER
How do you mean
FRÄULEIN WERDENFELS
Did you write the chapter on Edgar as a counter-chapter
to the chapter on Robert or was that
a secondary consideration
in relation to Professor Stieglitz
HERR MEISTER
An interesting question
In integrating Edgar into the structure I also took account
of the danger
threatening Robert through Edgar
The typology of Edgar
can be related to Robert's despair
that was a stylistic problem
in relation to Professor Stieglitz

if that is what you mean
I had a profoundly moving experience at Knossos
I don't have to say what Knossos means to me
since you're reasonably thoroughly acquainted with my oeuvre
I interpreted a legal inscription that had been found in Gortyn
differently from Sir Evans
and I interpreted it correctly because I approached my interpretation
from the correct premises
Evans from completely false ones
but you can read all that in my tetralogy
it will be very interesting for you very instructive
Minoan culture plays a most important role in my tetralogy
it necessitated going to Crete twice
for a longish stay
above all for the chapter on Edgar
of course the chapter on Edgar can only be understood
if you understand Knossos
but then only if you have come to my conclusions
and not to Sir Evans's conclusions
for me that was the most exciting work
I have ever done
it took me years of unbroken concentration
to bring the Edgar chapter to final completion
of course my wife helped me a lot with it
I have much to thank my wife for in every sense
FRÄULEIN WERDENFELS
    Regarding Book One and Book Two
    the leading critics maintain
    you have used some of Edgar's traits
    I mean Edgar's character traits
    in Robert as well
    in general that the chapter on Robert has a lot of Edgar in it
    is that true I mean can that be true
HERR MEISTER
    Naturally something of Robert has gone into Edgar Fräulein
    Werdenfels

and something of Edgar a not inconsiderable amount into
Robert
still it surprises me that the critics are capable of such
perception
it genuinely surprises me
most of them simply do not possess the ability
to come to a profound understanding of a work of art
everything about them is superficial everything
it just so happens that here the critics have happened to see
what the philosophical connection is
between Edgar's perspective *on* nature
and Robert's philosophy of art
But of course only two critics have seen that
and we agree I'm sure that with these two
we are dealing with the best in the field
but even those two got things wrong for decades
If the critics had been right
I would have killed myself long ago
but each time I managed to conquer my depression
I engaged with my subject that is all
the creative artist above all the literary artist
the writer must engage with his subject
everything else is unimportant
Stieglitz says in the fifth chapter
he must listen to himself
to nothing else
my Professor Stieglitz says
It is not only the critics that are dire in Germany
They praise and they condemn
and they know not what they are praising
and what they are condemning
they have no comprehension at all of what they are dealing
with
as Stieglitz says
the sooner a creative artist realizes that the better
of course the young the developing artist
is at the mercy of these critics

the critics have destroyed many a genius before now
but new ones will keep on coming
as long as the world still stands
geniuses are an integral part of nature too
Myself I have developed a thick skin
and I keep my eyes fixed on the work in question
today I can't complain
nor can Stieglitz in my tetralogy
he has the world at his fingertips if you understand what I
mean
for years now everything that has been written about me has
been positive
since my sixty-fifth birthday not a single hurtful word
whenever I see my name in the paper
it's always followed by respectful praise
it spurs one on of course
if I had had such a response earlier
who knows what I might not have achieved
FRÄULEIN WERDENFELS
How would you characterize your relationship to nature
is it as you say a pure natural relationship
or pure something else as Professor Stieglitz says
HERR MEISTER
I cannot say it is a pure natural relationship
it is a lifelong interest
in things in matter
and in the philosophy which has that as its purport
you understand
mine is a mathematical destiny
it is completely bound up with nature
it is in every one of my poems
it is in every piece of prose
it is in everything in which I have my being
FRÄULEIN WERDENFELS
Why is the chapter on Robert shorter than the chapter on
Edgar

HERR MEISTER

It is connected with mathematics
and with statics
and with archaeology
It was determined by my Knossos experience
it is the way my Professor Stieglitz's world vision takes in the
cosmos
But I don't have the time just now
to go into this problem in detail
a very interesting question
I have never been asked it before
But then I have never discussed the tetralogy as a whole with
anyone
apart from you
apart from my wife of course
The Edgar chapter has something to do with Beethoven's *Fifth*
the Robert chapter with Schoenberg's *Moses and Aaron*
but that would be taking us too far

FRÄULEIN WERDENFELS

It is striking the way you suddenly invert the time problem

HERR MEISTER

Well you see

FRÄULEIN WERDENFELS

Why between the Edgar chapter and the Robert chapter
In the next room Frau Meister starts to play a Chopin fantasy, very
quietly

HERR MEISTER

Well you see that is my philanthropy
that is my egos my matala as Stieglitz says

FRÄULEIN WERDENFELS

Yes your matala

HERR MEISTER

You do know what matala is

FRÄULEIN WERDENFELS

Yes of course

HERR MEISTER

My matala my matala

What is at issue is common sense
is the power of disposal Stieglitz says
So easy for Zeus to be in the way isn't it
FRÄULEIN WERDENFELS
The cause was surely your relationship
to the incompatibilities as you once put it
HERR MEISTER
Certainly oh certainly
There is a fairy tale the fairy tale is called Tobias
in that fairy tale you can read up everything
concerning the Robert chapter
and when you have understood that
the Edgar chapter will be clear to you as well
it's not mere chance that it's on a first of
January that my Professor Stieglitz goes from Kabul to
Teheran
But why have we only been talking
about these two chapters
My tetralogy has four hundred and twenty-eight chapters
if I am not very much mistaken
and the most important one is without doubt the one
in which Professor Stieglitz travels through Afghanistan
FRÄULEIN WERDENFELS
I intend to concentrate on those two chapters
in my thesis
On the one hand on the Edgar chapter
because of the wealth of concepts of the logos if for nothing
else
on the other on the Robert chapter
because of its anthroposophy
HERR MEISTER
Yes that will be it probably
*looks towards the next room from which the piano music is coming slightly
more loudly*
How beautifully my wife plays
she is a great virtuoso
You should know that in truth

her mother was an archduchess
a Habsburg you should know
but we don't talk about that
very softly
although it is a truth we appreciate
the piano music stops
FRAU MEISTER *comes into the library and announces*
Herr von Wegener has just arrived
HERR MEISTER *surprised*
Oh he has
stands up
to Fräulein Werdenfels
A gentleman from the *Frankfurter Allgemeine Zeitung*
who wants to write an article about me
Fräulein Werdenfels stands up
a nice young man
from the Black Forest
with delightful manners
FRAU MEISTER
Still available Fräulein Werdenfels
from an excellent family

SCENE FIVE

Dining room
Herr and Frau Meister, Fräulein Werdenfels and Herr von Wegener
having lunch
HERR MEISTER
The finds that were made in Phaestos
are much more imposing than those from Knossos
Knossos is disappointing
Evans did more harm than good to the finds
It's astonishing how long that man
nothing more than a madman working on the Queen's behalf
went on causing havoc there
On the other hand Knossos attracts far more interest

than Phaestos not to mention Ayía Triadha
FRAU MEISTER
> For me it's not just the finds
> the scenery has always been important to me as well
> Of course my husband finds that depressing

HERR MEISTER
> My wife always talks about bits of old pottery
> when she talks about the finds
> no this science is a closed book
> to the layman
> archaeology is not for the layman
> Stieglitz says

FRAU MEISTER
> My husband is working on a paper
> on Knossos with special reference
> to Ayía Triádha
> *addressing her husband directly*
> Now that you've finished the tetralogy
> you can devote yourself fully to your archaeological paper

HERR MEISTER
> Even as an adolescent I was interested in Schliemann
> I devoured everything Schliemann had written
> *Frau Herta, the cook, comes in and pours wine for everyone*

FRAU MEISTER
> It's absurd isn't it
> that Evans believed all Minoans
> were the same height
> namely no more than five foot tall

HERR MEISTER
> The thought that one is walking on the very same stones
> where King Minos walked
> Now of course the most valuable pieces
> from the museum in Herakleion have been sold to places all
> over the world
> as always of course almost everything of value has been
> grabbed
> by the Americans

one has to go to New York
to examine the most valuable pieces
addressing Fräulein Werdenfels directly
I always admired the scholarly work your father wrote
about Troy
Accompanying your father to Troy
must have made some decisive, existentially decisive
impressions on you
FRÄULEIN WERDENFELS
Yes of course
it was unforgettable
HERR MEISTER
How long is it since your father died did you say
FRÄULEIN WERDENFELS
Four years
he died of pneumonia
HERR MEISTER
As Professor Stieglitz says
it's an honor for a scholar
to perish in the course of his scholarly work
He caught cold on the Acropolis if I'm not mistaken
FRÄULEIN WERDENFELS
Yes the winter of seventy-six
HERR MEISTER
But he had already completed his book on Troy hadn't he
FRÄULEIN WERDENFELS
Yes he caught the cold just as it was finished
and three weeks later he was dead
HERR MEISTER
Medical science always fails
But when it's over it's over
isn't that so Herr von Wegener
How is your mother
is her liver still giving her problems
HERR VON WEGENER
Her pancreas Herr Professor
since childhood

HERR MEISTER

> That is terrible
> I had a great aunt who had problems with her pancreas
> I did not envy her at all
> she couldn't eat any of the things we ate
> Medical science is still in its infancy
> And your father how is Professor von Wegener

HERR VON WEGENER

> Last spring he led an expedition to the Arctic

FRAU MEISTER

> Eighteen people died on it didn't they

HERR VON WEGENER

> Yes through human error
> The navigator made a mistake

FRAU MEISTER

> How dreadful to die
> in the Arctic don't you think
> To perish in the eternal ice
> We even thought your father was among the victims
> but then we breathed a sigh of relief when we heard
> he was all right

HERR MEISTER

> People always underestimate the Arctic
> above all young people underestimate the Arctic
> Nansen Sven Hedin they were real men
> but those days are past
> We have the young people at our table the people of today
> *raises his glass to Fräulein Werdenfels*
> and such a pretty young lady
> such a charming scholar
> it's very rare
> that looking at a real a genuine scholar
> can give one such pleasure in being alive
> *they all raise their glasses and drink*
> Oh is life not beautiful
> among young people says Stieglitz
> We have always been on the side of youth

the older we grow the more intensive our
contact with young people
Of course the youth of today has its dark side too
we've all heard of degenerate youth
but of course you two are the pure embodiment of youth
My wife and I are open to youth
we trust young people they are our future
as my Professor Stieglitz says
HERR VON WEGENER
What a magnificent house this is
HERR MEISTER
It is the house of a Jew
emigrated to America driven out by the Nazis
but those were times you know nothing about
you can know nothing about those terrible times
just be glad you know nothing about them
terrible times weren't they Anne
finishes off the wine in his glass
A merchant of Jewish origin
like my Professor Stieglitz
A benefactor of this city
like my Professor Stieglitz
well educated highly cultured people
like my Professor Stieglitz
emigrated to Portugal first then to the United States
a true Jewish fate wasn't it Anne
like my Professor Stieglitz
My God evil times abysmal times
After the war the people didn't return to Germany
they made a present of this house to the city
they did not want to have anything more to do with Germany
like my Professor Stieglitz
For a long time the city used it to house visitors
its situation is just too beautiful
it was built with exquisite taste
the man who built it must have had great taste
The Jewish problem is still a dreadful problem

there will never be a solution
There are many things that are the Jews' own fault
the Jews are to blame for many things
but what was done to them should not have been done
yet at every hole and corner one is still reminded
of this terrible guilt of the Germans

FRAU MEISTER

We knew lots of Jews
all very nice people
but of course there were many very many
who positively asked to be exterminated

HERR MEISTER

The annihilation of the Jews was a big mistake
But it was an insoluble problem

HERR VON WEGENER

Did you leave this house the way it was

HERR MEISTER

We left it as it was
Sometimes we still think even today of those people
who built it
we are reminded of them at every step
But on the other hand one cannot spend all one's time raking
up the past
that's not what we want
the Germans and the Jews will always hate each other
Professor Stieglitz says in my tetralogy
Frau Herta comes in and pours wine for them all

FRAU MEISTER

Power's always been in the hands of the Jews

HERR MEISTER

Of course the Jews have always pulled the strings
It is the Jew who decides Stieglitz says
it is the Jew who has his hand on the tiller
even if that's not what it looks like
it is the Jew who has his hand on the tiller
All the important positions in the world are in the hands of the
Jews

even today
Where there's wealth you'll find the Jew
where there's beauty you'll find the Jew says Stieglitz
HERR VON WEGENER
    The house is certainly built on an ideal spot
HERR MEISTER
    You see
only a Jew could have built this house
such generosity of spirit such openness of mind
HERR VON WEGENER
    It is beautifully situated in the landscape
HERR VON MEISTER
    For an epicure certainly
HERR VON WEGENER
    As I was coming up to the house I thought
how well things have turned out for you
it must have been a happy chance
that the city placed this house at your disposal
HERR MEISTER
    At first we were unsure whether to accept it
because it seemed too large for us
and then also because it had been Jewish property
and then we moved in after all
FRAU MEISTER
    And now we've become so used to it
we can't imagine
moving away
if only because of the theater and the opera
It's also important for my husband's health
to live here
because of his weak lung
It's only here he could have written the tetralogy
HERR MEISTER
    I think so too
in all these ideal conditions
FRAU MEISTER
    Above all we are completely undisturbed here

well away from the noise and the stench
HERR MEISTER
> We live a quiet life up here
> but not shut off no
> not shut off from what is going on in the world
> We take all the important newspapers
> and we have very good television reception

FRAU MEISTER
> At first we were against it
> but then we felt it was necessary
> not to be completely shut off from world events
> but we only watch things that really interest us

HERR MEISTER
> It is a question of discipline
> one can always switch off after all

FRAU MEISTER
> And since my husband has started making frequent
> appearances on the screen
> it's become necessary of course
> *Frau Herta serves second helpings of meat*
> What would I do without you Frau Herta
> Saved
> *to the others*
> Frau Herta is a real treasure
> she lives with her family just on the other side of the wood
> she's such a bundle of energy
> Her husband drives a tractor for the electricity company
> The house would be too much for me to manage on my own
> There are such delightful people round here
> we get on well with them all
> above all with the simple folk
> My husband has a good way with the people here
> after all he comes from the area and knows them through and
> through
> and by now I feel I belong here too

FRAU HERTA
> When can I serve the dessert Frau Professor

FRAU MEISTER
> When I ring Frau Herta
> when I ring
> *Frau Herta goes out*
> We have a very genuine relationship
> with the simple folk

HERR MEISTER
> As does Professor Stieglitz

FRAU MEISTER
> You have to have that if you live in the country
> We're neither of us complicated my husband and I
> When there's a need we step in and lend a hand
> But tell us about your trip to India Fräulein Werdenfels
> what was it like there
> did you find the climate bearable
> My husband and I are wondering whether it is not too late
> to go to India
> at our age it's not something to be undertaken lightly
> How long did you spend in Calcutta

FRÄULEIN WERDENFELS
> We were there for six weeks

FRAU MEISTER
> Six whole weeks
> The poverty there

FRÄULEIN WERDENFELS
> We had only planned to stay for three days
> but my uncle fell ill
> with dysentery
> and he had to go to the hospital

FRAU MEISTER *horrified*
> A hospital in Calcutta
> horrific

FRÄULEIN WERDENFELS
> He had to share a room with four others
> you can't imagine
> the conditions there
> it's bad enough out in the streets

in the hospitals
it's absolutely unbelievable
FRAU MEISTER
My nephew Traugott the banker
died in an Indian hospital in Benares
before the war just imagine
the conditions in India must have been even worse in those
days
they still had an English viceroy
India was still a colony
HERR MEISTER
And was it dysentery
FRÄULEIN WERDENFELS
The doctors said it was dysentery
FRAU MEISTER
Then your uncle must have lost a lot of weight
FRÄULEIN WERDENFELS
He was nothing but skin and bones
HERR MEISTER
Of course you mustn't drink the water in India
that is the first rule
don't drink the water or eat salad
HERR VON WEGENER
Not in Italy either
HERR MEISTER
Not south of the Alps
and certainly not in Asia
When we were in Egypt we didn't drink the water
or eat salad
that goes without saying
But it must have been quite an experience mustn't it
a hospital in Calcutta
FRAU MEISTER
And your uncle came out again
FRÄULEIN WERDENFELS
That was the miracle
we had intended to stay in India for two months

but when my uncle was discharged from the hospital
we came back to Europe
FRAU MEISTER
That kind of thing always does lasting damage
FRÄULEIN WERDENFELS
He made a good recovery
In Switzerland
in the Engadine
HERR MEISTER
On a chocolate diet I assume
they all laugh and drink
FRAU MEISTER
My husband has always wanted
to travel to India
once it was even arranged
a magazine had offered to finance the trip
but then my husband got cold feet
after all India is very dangerous
anywhere you go in India you are exposed to the greatest
danger
once you are over fifty any trip to Asia is a risk
HERR MEISTER
It would have been more important anyway
to go to Persia again
Persepolis on the Persian Gulf
FRAU MEISTER
Once we thought of going to Burma
we knew someone from Burma
who'd invited us to go there
but then cholera broke out in Burma
HERR MEISTER
Disease is the great enemy of world travel
my Professor Stieglitz says
Disease or war
Europeans he says
feel the urge to go to Asia
to the most ancient cultures

FRAU MEISTER

    On another matter entirely Fräulein Werdenfels
    do please take a hot-water bottle
    if it's too cold for you in your room
    the guest room is on the north side unfortunately
    You said you'd caught a slight cold
    my husband and I are not used
    to sleeping in a warm bedroom
    we keep the windows open at night
    so that we always have fresh air
    but of course it all depends on what you're used to
    It can get really cold up here in the vineyards
    to Herr von Wegener
    Herr von Wegener is it true
    that my husband's essay on the nature of art of all the arts
    was published in the *Neue Zürcher Zeitung* in an abridged version
    I find it outrageous
    that they should cut a section
    mutilating the whole essay
    rendering it worthless

HERR VON WEGENER

    Unfortunately I have to say that that is true

FRAU MEISTER

    It is incredible
    the things newspapers think they can get away with
    rings for Frau Herta
    But one is powerless completely at their mercy
    all the newspapers print what they want in the form they want
    on the other hand if it wasn't printed at all
    whichever way you look at it
    puts a piece of bread in her mouth
    Last summer we were in Rome
    my husband gave a lecture in the Cultural Institute
    nothing literary pure science
    we were also received by the Pope
    a private audience
    My husband was awarded a papal decoration

Rome is such a magnificent city
we were guests of the state
we're guests of the state abroad as well
in all the bookshops we found
books by my husband Italian translations
Frau Herta comes in with a layer cake and serves it
Most of all I was fascinated
by the Sistine Chapel
and Michelangelo of course
The expressive power the dignity
I prefer Roman art to Greek
But I was so disappointed by St. Peter's
certainly the papacy is a great thing
The Pope seemed tired to me fatigued
overburdened
he talked to us for half an hour just imagine
He wanted to know how high the Großglockner was
my husband could tell him right away
He was wearing such beautiful buckled shoes all in white
I thought at first it was leather
but then I saw it was silk
buckled shoes of pure silk
There is something really royal about the Pope's face
Just think what that man has taken upon himself
waves Frau Herta over and whispers in her ear, then
This cake is called St. Cecilia's cake
why I don't know
Fräulein Werdenfels gets up to take a photo of them all
our grandmother used to make it on St. Cecilia's day
Mozart composed a mass for St. Cecilia's day didn't he
HERR VON WEGENER *wagging his finger*
Haydn Haydn
FRAU MEISTER
My husband loves his St. Cecilia's cake
to her husband
You love St. Cecilia's cake don't you
come on admit you love it

in a whisper
Actually he has a very sweet tooth
like his Professor Stieglitz
turning to address her husband directly
That's right isn't it
a very sweet tooth
Fräulein Werdenfels takes a photo with flash from the background

SCENE SIX

As in the previous scene
All eating cake, drinking coffee
HERR MEISTER
You know Herr von Wegener
a work that is still unfinished is like glass
the slightest carelessness and it breaks
says my Professor Stieglitz while traveling across Portugal by
train
Eluard Mallarmé Baudelaire Rimbaud
Goethe Novalis to a certain extent Heine of course
Hermann Hesse absolutely essential reading
perhaps I can mention Mörike too
Droste-Hülshoff Droste definitely Stieglitz says
But I had to be wary of the Romantics
The German can very quickly become sentimental
says Stieglitz to the pianist Gieseschwind
But it was primarily music I occupied myself with
first music and only then literature
I kept coming back to the classical period
I mustn't forget Wieland
and of course Klopstock made
a great impression on me
Frau Meister serves him a huge piece of cake
I love Klopstock
Do you love Klopstock Herr von Wegener
and you Fräulein Werdenfels

And Platen of course
just like Stieglitz
in fact for a long time I had a weakness for Stefan George
Slim and pure as a gem-like flame you know
Stieglitz quotes the poem in Los Angeles
sticks a large piece of cake into his mouth, speaks with his mouth full
Hofmannsthal of course
The April breezes blow along the avenues
my wife's favourite poem
But do feel free to write that I started out quite a revolutionary
a furious voice attacking conditions in our country
like Stieglitz
that's the way young people are, isn't it
arrogant assertive rebellious revolutionary
One's initial phase
the rejection of existing conventions
as described by Stieglitz
and not only in politics as regards the state
but as regards art as well
especially literature
but never abusive you know
No those early works I don't deny them
There was a phase
when I did want to destroy them
but my wife the custodian of my oeuvre
prevented it
And of course Hamsun I devoured him
Hunger and *Mysteries*
But it was his last book that made the greatest impression on
me
On Overgrown Paths that was its title wasn't it
his wife gives him another piece of cake
As far as the tetralogy is concerned
I threw out some suggestions to Fräulein Werdenfels
this morning
Suggestions are the most one can give
As a writer one restricts oneself to suggestions

one cannot explain one's own works
Stieglitz is simply a headword so to speak like cuckoo
one knows what it signifies but one cannot explain it
To be asked puts one in a very awkward position
One can ask a jam manufacturer
what is in his jam
but one can't ask a writer what is in his writing
That is so is it not Fräulein Werdenfels
It all has much to do with music
above all with symphonic music
I keep slipping in references to Beethoven
then I impel the various threads of the action to a conclusion
without using force
in the most natural manner
it's a process that stretches over decades
It is important that one feel no fear
One must not be afraid to get inside one's creation
on the other hand one must be prepared for everything
Feel free to write
that I have sacrificed my life to my art Herr von Wegener
that I have lived for my art alone
like Professor Stieglitz in my tetralogy
have taken everything upon myself
to advance my work to be able to complete it
what has always been important for me is the task in hand and
that alone
never anything else
so that the pleasure I got from life
was very limited
The kind of life other people lead
FRAU MEISTER
But you can't complain Moritz
to the others
My husband is a happy man you can write that
Herr von Wegener
he's not as gloomy as people think
they all keep writing that he's so gloomy

when there's no one who can be so jolly as my husband
Probably because people just can't imagine
that a writer a literary artist who writes serious things
can laugh
exclaims
And how my husband can laugh
You think so too don't you Fräulein Werdenfels
now that you know my husband
The newspapers are always writing about a Mr. Gloomy
and my husband's anything but gloomy
I couldn't have stayed with the kind of man the newspapers
describe
for one single day
to her husband
You aren't gloomy are you Moritz
HERR MEISTER
I am quite different
from the way I'm portrayed of course
there is certainly much of me in Stieglitz
But the portrayal is always different
As a writer one is always different from the way one is
portrayed
one is never the person the papers write about
They want a gloomy writer
so I must be a gloomy person
exclaims
The person portrayed is a fake
When the book laughs
the author is crying
and vice versa
again and again vice versa all the time
and a fake says Stieglitz
FRÄULEIN WERDENFELS
You put that so beautifully Herr Professor
HERR MEISTER
Who other than the writer the poet
can shape the word and raise it to beauty Goethe says

I think Goethe put that very beautifully
everyone can find strength in Goethe
he is the real the true poet of the Germans
The Germans admire his universal mind
Just imagine Kleist as our prince of poets
completely and utterly impossible
a suicide as Germany's prince of poets
The true prince of poets is Goethe the universal man
as Stieglitz says in Silvaplana
There is much of Goethe in each one of us
and that is how each one discovers his own genius
And of course I had great respect for mathematics
and for geometry of course
A work such as the tetralogy you know
is nothing other than geometry
mathematics is art is writing poetry genius
All roads lead to Goethe and from Goethe towards us
Goethe is the steady German
different from the English with their wild Shakespeare
The Germans like order not disorder
Goethe is the poet as philosopher
Shakespeare the poet as mystery
I showed that clearly in my tetralogy
there is the external geometry of the action
but what is infinitely more important is the inner geometry of
the mind
Schopenhauer who is absolutely not one of my favorite
philosophers says something similar
Nietzsche Schopenhauer those are the two antipodes of the
Germans
to Herr von Wegener
I have brought out the tragic aspect
in such a way that it does not spoil the enjoyment of the ideas
To let comedy arise out of tragedy
the comic realized in every idea so to speak
For them to progress demands an absolute lack of compromise
Your readers will surely be interested to read

that I worked on the tetralogy
for twenty-two years
that does not mean that other works were not written alongside
my major work
but all those so-called minor works
which I refuse to designate minor works
are naturally very important to me and remarkably all relate
to the tetralogy
It is marvelous that Fräulein Werdenfels
has seen that
turning to address Fräulein Werdenfels directly
I think you should bring that out in your thesis
namely that all the so-called minor works are related
to the tetralogy
everything points towards Stieglitz and is related to Stieglitz
it is a law of nature that all the works of one mind are related
to the major work of that mind
and the tetralogy is without a doubt my major work
That is my publisher's view as well
You'll meet him this evening
I will not part with the manuscript
even if he categorically demands it
as is his way
but I will read from it
a passage a short excerpt
the discussion between Stieglitz and Robert traveling on the
train across Portugal perhaps
possibly the conclusion
that is where it becomes crystal clear what I am doing in the
tetralogy
I have as you might say turned the story on its head
without infringing it in the least
The story as a natural process a kind of natural history
It is of course important that such a book
will be published by the most important publisher we have
who publishes only the best
addressing Herr von Wegener directly

It you want a photograph of me
there are only horrible photographs
FRAU MEISTER
We'll locate a good photo
Or why don't you use one of Fräulein Werdenfels's
There's a lovely half-length one of my husband
on a yacht leaning against the mast
in Kiel Herr von Wegener
on the President's yacht
at sunset it captures the atmosphere
in a way that's rarely achieved
The sun falls precisely on my husband's face
while the rest of his head is in darkness
very characteristic
they all finish their coffee

SCENE SEVEN

Outside
HERR MEISTER in a deck chair, signing books
FRAU MEISTER *observes him from the living room for some considerable time,*
then
You won't get your afternoon nap Moritz
How many books have you signed already today
Give it a rest
such a strenuous day
Herr von Wegener has gone for a walk in the vineyards with
Fräulein Werdenfels
Frau Herta's gone
her children have the measles
those children are always getting ill
whenever I ask about the children she says they're ill
everyone's always sickening for something round here
I don't understand it
when the air just here is so healthy
I've had a look through the mail nothing very exciting

You've been invited to go to Munich
they want you to give a reading in the Great Hall of the
University
something literary of your own choice
We ought to go to Munich again
I don't understand why we haven't been to Munich for such a
long time
after all it's the most essentially German city
biting into an apple
Now that you're famous
now that fame has caught up with you
The mayor rang up to ask
if we're going to his son's christening
I said yes my husband's finished with the tetralogy we can
come
next Tuesday
I've said yes for Mainz too
we ought to go to Karlsruhe as well
now that you've completed the tetralogy
The publisher coming at the right moment
What do you think of Fräulein Werdenfels
she'd be something for Herr von Wegener
perhaps I'll do a little matchmaking
they seem to me to suit each other well
from the same background from an academic milieu
I gave him some tips
for his article young Wegener
it'll all appear in a fortnight's time in the weekend edition
with the picture of you in Kiel
He'll take great care over it he says
a whole page perhaps more
He loves *Tannhäuser* too by the way
did you know his father was born on the eighth of December
as well
A bit weak don't you think
but they're all like that nowadays

goes over to her husband and takes the books away from him, first those he
has signed, then those he hasn't
People don't know what a burden they're placing on you
I sometimes wonder at their nerve
sending you books to be signed
when you don't know these people at all
takes the books into the house
HERR MEISTER wraps himself in a blanket and tries to sleep
Frau Meister comes back with a newspaper and says, standing in the
doorway
I think we ought to go to Munich
You're in good shape at the moment
and you've got the tetralogy out of the way
You can read from the tetralogy
It'll be a lovely trip
Not much in the way of luggage
and we'll stay at the Four Seasons
I can't understand why you don't like Munich
A walk in the English Garden after breakfast
sits down in a wicker chair
You've been so happy in Munich
It was Munich that made you
what you are today
you had your best years in Munich
Poverty and hardship of course
Evil The scum of the big city
but it was in the evil, the scum of the big city
that you developed
if you'd stayed here you wouldn't have got anywhere
without Munich you'd be nothing
The publisher is meeting us at the station
he's reserved the best rooms in the Four Seasons for us
we'll be received by the president of the university
and by the mayor of the city
and we'll be asked to sign the city visitors' book
you've done all that a hundred times before
The city as witness to your rise

you said that
Munich's not the same city it was twenty years ago
the city that treated you cruelly
nor are you the same as you were twenty years ago
You must get rid of this obsession
everything's changed since then and how
In those days you were nothing a man making his way
now you're famous
the famous writer elected to
the Academy for Language and Literature
Now I know what pride is Moritz
now's the time to go to Munich
to show them
Now they'll just stand and gawp at you
Uncle Vanya in the Residenz Theater do you remember
our first theater premiere
reads the newspaper
Not a day goes by but you're in the paper
I could bet on it every day and I'd win
Moritz Meister has been elected a member
of the Academy for Language and Literature
with this election the Academy's annual session
I keep wanting to read that sentence again and again
You're right I must control myself
puts the paper down
Are you going to go or are you not going to go
HERR MEISTER
    Only if they pay me three thousand marks
FRAU MEISTER
    You're getting three thousand
    plus expenses
    we won't have to spend a penny
HERR MEISTER
    I want it in writing
FRAU MEISTER
    I've already signed the contract
    your fame is worth three thousand to them

and they'll put you up at the Four Seasons
at their expense and me too of course your wife
gets up and goes over to her husband and kisses him on the cheek
For you because you're the greatest
You've surpassed them all
first caught up with them then left them behind
The arts sections of the papers are yours to command
my Moritz's
Moritz Meister Member of the Academy
and the President of Germany sends his congratulations
Oh yes
looks across towards the vineyards
HERR MEISTER
The struggle to get to the top was agony
from nothing from less than nothing
like my Professor Stieglitz
FRAU MEISTER
Of course my dear
Making your way was terrible

SCENE EIGHT

Library
HERR MEISTER, *Herr von Wegener, Fräulein Werdenfels*
HERR MEISTER *holding a large vase*
A copy it is true
but still a copy of the Harvesters' Vase from Ayía Triádha
look
Herr von Wegener and Fräulein Werdenfels move closer and look at the vase
What is everything that comes after this
everything is in this art
everything that was created later is nothing
You'll find the original in the museum in Herakleion
a pinnacle of art
that will never be reached again

Goethe wrote a profound essay on this vase
A pity you don't know the essay
You can find everything in Goethe
everything that is worth knowing
Goethe was the universal mind
the logos universalis
Herr von Wegener and Fräulein Werdenfels put their heads close to the
vase
It was not easy to obtain this copy
puts the vase down on the floor against the wall
Of course the original means more to me
as it would to any honest mind
But of course I couldn't acquire
the original of the Harvesters' Vase
Now look at this
takes a fragment of pottery from a shelf and shows it to them
From the pre-palace period look
Evans wrote a description of this shard
which appeared in the publications of London University in
nineteen twenty-eight
caused quite a stir by the way
This shard is original
It cost me a fortune
the whole of my advance for the Germania novel to be precise
which by the way has just come out in a new edition
In this bowl the Minoans
preserved their olives
the olives that came from Messara
Evans believed this bowl was made two thousand four
hundred years
before Christ
One of my most valuable pieces
take it go on take it
Fräulein Werdenfels holds the pottery fragment first, then Herr von
Wegener, who gives it back to HERR MEISTER
What is man
counted in millennia

We are nothing Fräulein Werdenfels absolutely nothing
puts the pottery fragment back on the shelf
It is very risky simply keeping this shard
on the shelf like this
but I hate glass covers you know
Frau Herta is not allowed to dust these shelves
Frau Herta mustn't touch anything in here
When the President was here
in the spring
after the spring maneuvers which he attended
I gave him the shard to hold
he kept it in his hand for over half an hour
he was filled with immense admiration
of course these works of art are only for exceptional people
turns round and takes a leather-bound volume from the shelves
There you have the original edition of the *Menetekel* of
Garnichäus
a rarity
leafs through it
You know it don't you Fräulein Werdenfels
FRÄULEIN WERDENFELS
     Yes of course
HERR MEISTER
     Matter of course for an educated person
     to Herr von Wegener
     I'm sure you know the book as well
HERR VON WEGENER
     Possibly Herr Professor
     it's a long time since
HERR MEISTER
     One can't know everything
     puts the book back on the shelf
     I always tell young people
     it's good to acquire more and more knowledge
     but you have to keep something for later
     even when you're old you still don't know very much
     and when you're as young as the pair of you are

Won't you sit down
he sits down in the rocker, Herr von Wegener and Fräulein Werdenfels sit
down in armchairs
My publisher will arrive around seven
he's a punctual man
very cultured as you'll see
with an incredible understanding of art
A conversation with him's a pleasure
whatever topic you choose
he's thoroughly at home with it
a rare talent indeed
German publishers as is well known
are not by any means always the most intelligent of creatures
this one is an exception
After all he is the one who publishes the outstanding minds
Now you'll have the evidence of your own eyes
that we're not at all shut off from the world up here
It's rare though that I have the opportunity of a conversation
with such a cultured man
Finding this publisher was a stroke of good fortune
and pure chance like so much in life
I met him in a hotel in Zurich
when I was still a completely unknown author
he was looking for someone to play cards with skat
and approached me
clearly he was alone
I could play skat
fortunately I should add
and it was only gradually it turned out
that he was the important publisher
and I the important author
He was the first to recognize me for what I was
before I found him I was completely unknown
ignored I might almost say
he had an eye for my work
he raised it out of the darkness and into the light

FRÄULEIN WERDENFELS
> Where your work shines

HERR MEISTER
> In actual fact I owe a great deal of my fame
> to my publisher
> You know Zurich is a city
> that has always brought me good fortune
> as it does my Professor Stieglitz as well
> It brought me together with my publisher
> It brought much into my life that must remain private
> I can't count how many things
> it all makes Zurich the city I love above all
> everyone has his favorite city
> In fact Switzerland in general has been a place of destiny for
> me
> I love Switzerland
> my wife can't understand it
> but that's very female
> Switzerland is not a country for the female taste
> a man's country certainly a man's country

FRÄULEIN VON WERDENFELS
> How did you get the idea
> of making Robert speak in Edgar's language
> in chapter eight
> while in chapter nine Edgar speaks in Robert's language
> I would call that a stroke of genius Herr Professor
> Where it suddenly switches to Robert's language
> or Edgar's tones

HERR MEISTER
> You know if I were to say anything about that
> which naturally I cannot
> my whole concept would fall apart in retrospect
> I can't tell you why should I
> The work is completed and will make its own way
> Let other people rack their brains over it now
> as many people as possible
> *to Herr von Wegener*

It's above all the foreign section of your newspaper that I
admire
of course there are things to criticize about all papers
but still the *Frankfurter Allgemeine* has
the most intelligent team of foreign correspondents of all
German newspapers
don't you agree
HERR VON WEGENER
Yes I think so too Herr Professor
HERR MEISTER
The reviews section is more debatable
all review sections are debatable
but possibly that of the *Frankfurter Allgemeine* more than most
You don't object to my saying that do you
HERR VON WEGENER
But not at all Herr Professor Meister
HERR MEISTER
My fate is in the hands of the newspapers and that's a fact
if newspapers didn't exist then neither would I
I think every writer can say that of himself
if he's honest
If the review section didn't exist
there wouldn't be any writers
It's a good review section they say
when they are praised in it
a poor one
if they are criticized
it's as simple as that
One moment please
gets up and takes a fat tome from the shelf and sits down again
My grandfather gave me this
A book that only appeared in an edition of three copies
in nineteen hundred and twenty-three I think
It's called *The Funnel*
an absolute rarity
The two other copies were destroyed by their owners
because they were unhappy with the content

the book is neither obscene nor the opposite
it just describes the two people
who destroyed their copies
and with good reason as you will see
if you read the book
But you won't be able to read the book
since I'm not going to let anyone have it
and before I die
I'm going to destroy it
A nice idea don't you think
Make a note of the title *The Funnel*
and the author's called Manuel Leiterstrasser
gets up, after he has leafed through it, puts the book back on the shelf and turns round
Leiterstrasser
sounds very Swiss to me
doesn't it

SCENE NINE

Drawing room
Frau Meister playing Liszt on the grand piano
Fräulein Werdenfels and Herr von Wegener sitting down
FRAU MEISTER *after she has stopped playing*
It isn't easy
being married to a celebrity
It's not for nothing my husband has a reputation for being
difficult
My husband is difficult I have to say
He's always been difficult
But you get used to it with time
And please Herr von Wegener put in your article that my
husband was awarded the papal Order of St. Sylvester
I've always been faithful to my husband
I stood by him even in the worst times
Times were hard for us during the first decades

we'd broken with everyone
even with our closest relations
it was necessary for my husband's development
An artist has to make his way alone
not looking to the right or the left
as Professor Stieglitz says
And the difficulties there were in Germany
Very often my husband threatened to commit suicide
even today he still keeps his pistol underneath his pillow
for years I was afraid he'd put a bullet through his head
he kept threatening he would
he'd kill himself he said if things went on as they were
But please don't put that in your article Herr von Wegener
Of course we've had happy times together as well
plays a few bars
Young days are always happy days
Then of course I gave up my art for his art
that is the most difficult thing
the one sacrifices himself for the other
we moved here and there all round Germany
all round Europe
but my husband's attached to his fatherland
not the kind to emigrate abroad you understand
Oh you don't know what it means Fräulein Werdenfels
to be married to a scientist or artist
to be married to a genius
But our modest expectations saw us through time and time
again
Our frugality
As you can see we live a very simple life up here
Thirty years what am I saying thirty-five years with no response
whatsoever
Then all at once success with the Germania novel
the press had woken up to him
But fame brings its problems too
Sometimes my husband finds it annoying
when they see in him the famous writer alone and nothing else

they forget he's a human being too
my husband believes in humanity
FRÄULEIN WERDENFELS
It must have been of great help to your husband
to be invited to Berlin by the Senate
FRAU MEISTER
Yes that was of great help to him
Suddenly the state was taking note of him
Look at this
*gets up, takes the large photo of the German President from the piano and
holds it up to the light*
The President
Signed and with a dedication in his own hand
The President has used his influence for him
he said he knew of no greater writer in Germany
and that when he was asked who he thought was the most
important German-language writer
he always said HERR MEISTER without having to stop to think
puts the photo back on the piano
My husband has a horror of publicity
he hates receptions
but he still attends them
he doesn't like giving readings
he has to be dragged to them kicking and screaming
but he gives them
He hates power Fräulein Werdenfels
sits down at the piano again
Money isn't important to him
but he doesn't condemn it either
nor is success important to him
but he doesn't run away from it oh no
He loves his readers Fräulein Werdenfels
Those serious illnesses my husband had
then the phase of psychiatric treatment you know about
the psychiatrists said to my husband
go to the south where it's warm
where the air's still unspoilt

But we couldn't do that
because my husband as a German writer
is tied to the lands where German is spoken
so we moved to south Germany
and what more natural
than to go to the area where my husband came from
Of course it could have all gone wrong
but then the city offered us this house
A suggestion from his publisher
and the city offered us this house
At first it was too big for us
too luxurious
and also because it had belonged to Jews
but then we decided to accept after all
and soon came to feel it was ideal
My husband wouldn't have written the tetralogy
if we hadn't moved to this house
from the very beginning it inspired my husband
one evening he went round all the rooms
from top to bottom then from bottom to top
took a deep breath and said
Now I'm going to make a start on the tetralogy
And from that moment on he worked on the tetralogy
The breath of this house has gone into the tetralogy
the breath of Professor Stieglitz
We're not shut off from cultural life
It's not far to go to the opera
my husband needs the opera
he can't live without an opera house
though we have very much reduced the number of times we go
to the opera
We have an excellent company here
outstanding guest singers
And then my husband had the idea of keeping bees
he's loved bees ever since he was a child
as has Professor Stieglitz
he built the bee-house himself

he's a very good craftsman you know
you can that every time he picks up a tool
his family background
as you know his father was a master carpenter
that's why my husband has always got on excellently
with the working class
but that's usually ignored
The newspapers always write
that my husband is completely self-centered
when he is entirely focused on the people
something quite exceptional in a man for whom the mind is
everything
FRÄULEIN WERDENFELS
  Hasn't your husband written a geometry textbook
FRAU MEISTER
  Yes of course
  it's well known among specialists
  and valued
  but all that stays in the dark
FRÄULEIN WERDENFELS
  Family background is the decisive factor
FRAU MEISTER
  Yes of course
  I made heavy weather of things Fräulein Werdenfels
  because of the milieu I come from
  But our shared love of art and literature above all
  bridged all differences
  Of course it isn't easy coming from a well-off family
  a family with very high expectations
  to marry someone from the working class
  even if he is an artist a writer
  But I realized what was in my husband immediately
  I saw it straight away at first sight
  and with time it proved to be true
  although of course it took decades
  before the world recognized it
  plays a few bars of Liszt

HERR VON WEGENER
> Liszt in Weimar
> an awkward situation wasn't it Frau Meister
> Wagner on the one side
> Liszt on the other

FRAU MEISTER
> I love Liszt
> I love his music
> I understand his music
> Liszt the man I cannot understand

HERR VON WEGENER
> Bülow Wagner Liszt Mathilde Wesendonk
> a very German constellation don't you think
> incommensurable

FRAU MEISTER
> The interpretative artist
> as my husband would say
> who ventures into the presence of the creative artist
> and is destroyed by the creative artist

HERR VON WEGENER
> A tragic constellation certainly

FRAU MEISTER *playing quietly*
> Very tragic
> tragic and romantic

HERR VON WEGENER
> Quintessentially German

FRAU MEISTER
> In some respects

HERR VON WEGENER
> The Hungarian soul and the German
> as a symbiosis a musical symbiosis

FRAU MEISTER
> I cried
> as I walked round Liszt's house in Weimar
> it was almost unbearable
> I felt I was going to suffocate
> it was only when I got back to Goethe and Schiller

that it went away
closes the piano lid
The lives of German artists are all much too tragic
HERR VON WEGENER
That brings Kierkegaard to mind
Enten Eller
Either Or
even in the north a man desperately seeking after the truth like
that
while here we have Liszt as philosopher
as moral philosopher aesthetic thinker and despairing human
being
I think your husband's relation to Kierkegaard
has made him the extraordinary man
he is today
Somewhere in the Germania novel it says
My Copenhagen of the mind
FRAU MEISTER
Professor Stieglitz says that in the tetralogy as well
HERR VON WEGENER
And from there it's not far to Strindberg
turning to address Fräulein Werdenfels directly
Is it Fräulein Werdenfels
FRÄULEIN WERDENFELS
Yes I think so too
I very much think so
HERR VON WEGENER
We turn a blind eye to the apocalypse says Meister
instead of focusing on it
we turn a blind eye to it
that is the tragedy of the Germans
FRAU MEISTER *getting up from the piano*
Very beautifully put Herr von Wegener

SCENE TEN

The library
The Publisher looks at the shelves and reads various titles; he takes a
volume out then puts it back, takes another volume out then puts that one
back
He examines the large vase and tries to pick it up, but gives up
immediately
He discovers a fragment of Cretan pottery and picks it up from the shelf.
At that moment HERR MEISTER can be heard calling out 'Anne' three
times
The Publisher puts the fragment back on the shelf
HERR MEISTER *enters with the beekeeper's veil over his head; even when he is*
in the library he still shouts out

Anne Anne
with a start of surprise
Oh it's you
you're here already
THE PUBLISHER *going over to HERR MEISTER*
The publisher is always punctual
they shake hands
HERR MEISTER
This is rather embarrassing
as you can see
I've got caught up in my veil
and my wife isn't here
tries to take the veil off
I've called her but she isn't around
I've no idea
tugging at the veil
where she is
PUBLISHER
Wait a minute
very carefully takes the veil off over HERR MEISTER's head
There you are
HERR MEISTER
The veil always gets caught up on the buttons

The Publisher has got the veil right off now
If I'd known
you were here already
Didn't my wife see you
PUBLISHER
She was just going
to tidy herself up a bit
HERR MEISTER
Well this is rather embarrassing
Please sit down do sit down
moves a chair for the Publisher, then another, then the armchair
Do please sit down
I have visitors
a young gentleman from the *Frankfurter Allgemeine*
a Herr von Wegener
perhaps you know him
and a young lady from Heidelberg a PhD student
nice people very nice people young and nice
PUBLISHER *sits down*
The price of fame
HERR MEISTER
Yes fame
PUBLISHER
It's young people above all who are reading your books
wherever I go
the first question I'm asked is always about the celebrated
Moritz Meister
Moritz Meister is a household name wherever books are read
Everyone is waiting for the tetralogy
Moritz is one of the most popular names just now
*HERR MEISTER notices that the vase is not in its correct position and
adjusts it*
The youth of this country are completely taken up with your
books
in a way they are with no one else's
they study them with passion and with the greatest academic
rigor

*HERR MEISTER glances at the pottery fragment and adjusts the position
of that as well*
That's the fantastic thing about these young people today
they take the very best works as their yardstick
So many dissertations on you
and on no one else
Have you read Lenk's article
Professor Lenk from Marburg
he deals with your Germania novel
profoundly imbued with your view of things
I've thought highly of Lenk for years
I encouraged him to write a book for us
on the spirit of our times
or rather their lack of it
My dear HERR MEISTER
I hope things have gone well
You know what I mean
HERR MEISTER
    I know
PUBLISHER
    The tetralogy
HERR MEISTER
    Is finished
    I have achieved the inconceivable
PUBLISHER
    There will be a massive response
    to your book
    we'll bring it out in a big edition
    worldwide
    let's say a hundred thousand copies
    perhaps a hundred and fifty thousand
    so many inquiries
    never before have there been so many inquiries
    And your election to the Academy of Language and Literature
    came just at the right moment
    and of course we get the spin-off
    from the fact that you're traveling all round Germany now

HERR MEISTER

Just one moment if you'll excuse me
just one moment
I'll be back right away
goes off
*The Publisher takes a piece of paper out of his inside jacket pocket, reads
it through, then puts it back again and looks round the library*
*He gets up, goes over to the pottery fragment again and looks at it, then
sits back down, stretches out his legs, draws them up then stretches them
out again*
HERR MEISTER *returns, hair combed and wearing a long grey cardigan;
he goes over to the drinks*
You'll let me offer you a glass of wine

PUBLISHER

Yes of course certainly
*HERR MEISTER fills two glasses and goes across to the Publisher, who
has stood up; they empty their glasses*
A very acceptable little wine

HERR MEISTER

We are very happy here my wife and I
they sit down
Everything was still undecided
when we moved in here
after all there was no guarantee
I could work here
to return to the place where you grew up is taking a great risk
However my wife was very keen to go somewhere
we could settle down
Now we are settled here
I have the healthy air
I have my bees
I have great enthusiasm for my work

PUBLISHER

The Academy has approached me
to ask you
whether you would give a lecture
on the novel the novel as such

it will of course be entirely up to you
how you tackle the subject
Since you've finished with the tetralogy now
well I thought
it would be extremely valuable to coincide with the appearance
of the tetralogy
you could put in an appearance too
at the next session of the Academy
one could say they're just waiting for you for nobody else
your appearance at the Academy
is seen as a sensation definitely

HERR MEISTER *leaning back*

In certain respects one could say
that I am free now
and I wouldn't find it too difficult
to undertake
a topic such as the one proposed
The novel the novel *as such* you said

PUBLISHER

Yes

HERR MEISTER

That could be exciting
I might just be in the mood for it
I could imagine
now after the tetralogy
after all those years of concentrating on Professor Stieglitz
throwing myself into a piece of scholarly work
to take my mind off him so to speak to give it something new
to focus on

PUBLISHER

My wife sends her warmest greetings
She'd be delighted honored
if you came to visit us again soon

HERR MEISTER

Yes now that I can suddenly breathe freely again
now after the tetralogy

PUBLISHER

> Things are looking promising
> the other books are selling well too
> no complaints things are looking up
> We've signed contracts with Scandinavia
> with Sweden which I consider very important
> ,with Norway and with Finland
> everything takes its time
> who would have thought five years ago
> that today you'd be a famous author in America
> it's astonishing how exactly you've hit
> your subject and your times
> it's not something you can plan can work out in advance
> The Sorbonne has inquired whether it would be possible
> for you to give a lecture there in the autumn
> in French
> You once indicated
> you might be interested in saying something about Voltaire
> with reference to your views on France
> or perhaps something about your Professor Stieglitz in relation
> to Voltaire
> But I don't want to push you
> a publisher shouldn't push
> just observe
> and wait

HERR MEISTER

> In a way I'm very much obliged to France
> When I was twenty I was translating Baudelaire
> but than I gave up translation
> because I formed the view it would harm my own work

PUBLISHER

> A great pity you gave up translation
> in particular the Baudelaire translations that are around
> are not good
> it annoys me every time I read Baudelaire in translation
> but of course I only read French authors in the original
> Baudelaire Verlaine Mallarmé Rimbaud Proust

leans back
The French authors all need new translations
but by whom that is the question
for years I've been searching for good translators
but I can't find any that are acceptable
HERR MEISTER
Proust for example has been translated two or three times
and each time they say what a brilliant translation
but after ten years at the most it turns out
that this brilliant translation is nothing more than an
amateurish effort
It's the same with Joyce
PUBLISHER
A publisher is always searching
for what is new
HERR MEISTER
A publisher is the conscience of the nation
PUBLISHER *looks round the library*
How things have changed here
over the last few years
Greatness I think that is greatness
Here is greatness
HERR MEISTER
There is room for a lot of things here
I never had room for before
above all my archaeological collection
PUBLISHER
Ah yes archaeology
my wife and I
are planning a trip to Mexico
and we intend to go to Peru as well
we'll come to you for all the background first
HERR MEISTER
Of course I'm not so familiar with
Latin-American history
PUBLISHER
At the moment we have some marvelous Latin-American

authors in our list
world authors all of them the best there are today
looking at the vase
How old is that vase
HERR MEISTER
    Two and a half thousand years before Christ roughly
PUBLISHER
    Impressive
    it must be immensely valuable then
HERR MEISTER
    It's a copy of course
    that goes without saying
    but I'm very attached to that vase
    I could not be without that vase
PUBLISHER
    The author must always be in touch
    with the whole of history
    if he loses touch with it
    even just for the briefest of moments
    his greatness is lost too
HERR MEISTER
    History and the author form
    a unity
PUBLISHER
    The thinking mind takes everything from history
    and history takes everything from the thinking mind
    that's Novalis I think
HERR MEISTER
    It could be Novalis
    but it's a sentence from my tetralogy
    spoken by Professor Stieglitz
    page eight hundred and three at the bottom
PUBLISHER *exclaims*
    Phenominacious
HERR MEISTER
    My greatest asset has always been
    a memory that stores information precisely

PUBLISHER

    In the autumn we're bringing out the Germania novel
in paperback
we've sold the rights to China
we're negotiating with Japan
Korea will go along with them
I think your future's in China

HERR MEISTER

    I always wished
I knew Chinese a wish that has remained unfulfilled

PUBLISHER

    My wife is getting quite excited at the idea
that you might do us the pleasure
with your wife
of going to England with us
It'll do you good
England that's a gap isn't it
you've never been to England have you

HERR MEISTER

    I've never been to England the land of Shakespeare

PUBLISHER

    We have a house in Cornwall
you could possibly even work there
You never know until you try
you might suddenly find you can even in a foreign country
what do you think

HERR MEISTER

    I have never been able to work in a foreign country
I've tried again and again
but I can't
no more than my Professor Stieglitz
I've always been tied to German to the land where German is
spoken
I thought I would be able to in Egypt for example
but then I couldn't
we were staying close to the pyramids
the ideal environment for writing I thought

but not one line nothing
of course the archaeologist inside me took over
the writer had to stand aside
PUBLISHER
    We'll travel light when we go to England
    The English air will do you good
HERR MEISTER
    I always feel depressed in France
PUBLISHER
    You definitely won't feel depressed in England
    I think you're a man for England
    you'll feel at home with the English character
    A publisher has a duty to make sure he takes his authors to places
    where they can be creative
    But you are so creative Meister
    so very creative
    I can't wait to read the tetralogy
    I've just been reading Kierkegaard
    he's a man I didn't know particularly well
    it was a revelation what a man
    A lot of things in Kierkegaard remind me of you
    There's a Kierkegaard inside you
    perhaps you don't realize it
    yes really a Kierkegaard
HERR MEISTER
    I have an affinity with Kierkegaard
    and with Strindberg
    to a certain extent
PUBLISHER
    I'm publishing Strindberg just now
    perhaps you'll write a preface
    for this edition
    That would be splendid
    We're publishing all the Nordic writers
    bit by bit
    exclaims

Ibsen what a mind
I went to Sweden a year ago
and found an unpublished work by Ibsen
A comedy
written *before Peer Gynt*
Phenominacious
I'm publishing it next year
with a collection of commentaries
By the way I'm planning a new series
something for young people for young people at the university
we could bring out your essay on the nature of the cosmic in it
I've got six manuscripts already
I'm looking for new editors
two are ill
one has died
I have to replace all these people from time to time
I'm looking for a young man
who has worked intensively on Wieland
do you know anyone
I'm trying to put a new Kant edition together
it's difficult
Kant who has entirely dominated
the German mind
Have you heard of Möbius
HERR MEISTER shakes his head
Möbius has written a book on moral philosophy
a quite exceptional work
I'm publishing it in the spring
And a lovely little thing by Engels completely unknown
a tender story basically a Christmas story
Everything is going well for the company
even if at the moment publishing in general
is in crisis
admittedly the book trade is in crisis
but I'm not affected by that not me
takes the piece of paper out of his jacket pocket
Things are looking good Meister

Your account is in balance
I find that very pleasing
We've sold eighty thousand of the Germania novel
Once the tetralogy has come out
we can hardly wait
such an important book at the right moment
Three volumes in a slipcase
bound in black as you requested
and with the subtitle
Stieglitz or the Ordering of the World
HERR MEISTER *gets up and pours more wine then sits down again*
There's a lot of talk of poor returns
but not as far as *we* are concerned
we're going along nicely
When the tetralogy comes onto the market
you'll have to give a few readings in Berlin too
no getting out of it
it's essential the author show himself
the public has a right to see the author
they need to see him in the flesh from time to time
puts the piece of paper away
As far as your election to the Academy is concerned
I pulled one or two strings myself
nothing happens of itself
Now everyone is waiting
for you to turn your hand to the theater
HERR MEISTER *shakes his head in disbelief*
A play you know
written by you
performed at one of the top theaters
with the best actors
the Hamburg Schauspielhaus for example
or the Schiller Theater in Berlin
HERR MEISTER
I have never felt the urge to write for the stage
but you never know

PUBLISHER
    A new German Shakespeare who knows
    Your books are absolutely exploding with drama
    there are so many dramas in your novels
    individual chapters in your Germania novel
    are like dramas
    remarkable
HERR MEISTER
    Some people have said that already
PUBLISHER
    Your works are bursting with drama
HERR MEISTER
    Who knows what the morrow will bring
PUBLISHER
    And of course in England
    you'll be walking in Shakespeare's footsteps
    and my wife and I will accompany you
    A German mind needs to spend some time
    in the English air
    looks round the library
    You have reestablished
    the tradition of this house
    The German mind owes almost everything
    to the Jews
    We need some more recent good photos of you
    I'll send a young photographer
    in the next few weeks
    a nice young man he won't be a nuisance
    Ten complimentary copies of the tetralogy will that be enough
HERR MEISTER
    Ten or twelve
PUBLISHER
    We'll send twelve
    we'll send fourteen
    It really is astonishing
    in Germany we suddenly have writers
    of European class again of world class

I'm talking about *two* writers you know who I mean
but when I'm here I think
you are the greatest
two such outstanding minds writing in German
dominating the world at the moment
but *your* oeuvre has its place assured is the greater
takes pride of place
authentic *German* writing of world quality
Everything in Germany rests on two writers
but even more on *your* works alone
You are definitely up there with Ibsen or Strindberg
if not far above both of them
what Strindberg is to drama
you are to prose
not a Goethe
a Strindberg of prose
What courage to tackle such a work
and what stamina to carry it to the peak of perfection
Alone ever onwards and upwards
How long did you actually spend working on the tetralogy
HERR MEISTER *has lit a pipe while the Publisher was speaking*
Twenty-two years to be precise
PUBLISHER
That is greatness
Twenty-two years
what a monumental achievement
In every word of your book you can feel
how it has been tried and tested weighed in the balance of the
mind
HERR MEISTER
Stieglitz or the Ordering of the World
it is immense
I have much to thank my wife for
For decades I had to depend on her alone
She gave up everything for me
everything almost everything
Whenever I was unsure she kept me going

She it was who guided me
without her I would be nothing
PUBLISHER
An existence reduced to the barest minimum
that alone allowed the work to develop naturally
so that now it stands before us firm well founded
imperishable
HERR MEISTER
I need the vineyard
I need peace
here I can concentrate
PUBLISHER
And a foray out into the world now and then
To the sites of classical antiquity
Persia Greece Egypt
you can sense it in every line of your works
it permeates
everything you have written
But the air at the summit is thin
HERR MEISTER
Very thin very thin
PUBLISHER *after a look round the library*
So I'll get to hear
something from the tetralogy this evening won't I
a sample yes
HERR MEISTER
I'll read from my tetralogy
In your honor
in honor of my publisher
Professor Stieglitz on the train traveling across Portugal
to Coimbra to his destination

SCENE ELEVEN

Drawing room
Everyone, including Frau Herta and the Mailman, sitting, some in

armchairs, others on ordinary chairs
HERR MEISTER *opposite them at a table, with a manuscript*
The curtain rises on applause
HERR MEISTER *after a longish pause during which he keeps leafing through his manuscript*

Now I will read another passage from the Edgar chapter this time
the end
Robert has come from Trieste
steeped in history The city in darkness the harbor deserted
Marlene hears nothing about his tragedy with Edmund
who has stayed in London
The affair with Cyrus is forgotten
The newspapers have decided that no more reports about Cyrus
will be published
The article Edgar spoke to Robert about
has not appeared because *The Times* does not print that kind of article
In Germany at this point there is a violent storm
Robert simply cannot accept
Edgar's decision
You must remember that Edgar was surprised that Robert
went to see Professor Stieglitz of his own free will and
was ready to sacrifice himself for the sake of his project
The reason he studied theology was to forget surgery
England was suffering from the effects of the weak pound
Thus Friedrich did not manage
to get hold of the newspaper with the report of Edgar's decision
contrary to the assumption made by Robert who had been certain
that Friedrich would see the newspaper
The ships were stuck in the harbor at Aden
Professor Stieglitz was suffering from a cold in Caracas
In London the prime minister himself had given orders
to stop negotiating with Stieglitz

The Queen was in New Zealand
Thus Friedrich was preparing for his trip to Mexico
though without any expectation of success
while at the same time Robert was still working on his plan
that very same plan that was to prove Edgar's undoing
fixing his gaze on his audience
if you need an explanation you'll find it in the Civil Code
Finally Robert went for a walk with Lynn in Central Park
and arranged to meet her in Oxford
Professor Stieglitz completed his book on Schopenhauer
Both were agreed the whole thing was impossible without
Edgar
But of course one can't talk of a conspiracy
At this point the style corresponds precisely to the content very
light very rhythmical largo
corresponding to the impossibility of ever again
recreating in England
the conditions Robert had dreamed of
and Edgar wanted to prevent
And Germany had not taken appropriate action
Stieglitz was absolutely persona non grata in Frankfurt
Fräulein Werdenfels takes a photo of HERR MEISTER with flash
In Germany everything went its sluggish inhuman way
roughly the same mood as in the Germania novel from chapter
five onward
there too of course the question of the times of time
The three-dimensional approach that allowed me to combine
the Edgar strand with the Robert chapter in the end
that is the Goethe Wittgenstein Kierkegaard constellation
But listen
pauses then starts to read
When Edgar arrived in Paris from London weary of America
there was no longer anything left to further his plan to
complete his project
he was filled with his love of Germany
but nonetheless he could not manage the move to England
Robert gave up his plan to travel to China thus neutralizing

the counter-standpoint of Edgar who had consulted Stieglitz
At this point it was strangely gray in Nice
Fräulein Werdenfels takes a photo of HERR MEISTER with flash
The sea was overshadowed by events in Central Europe
from which no initiative at all emerged
matters had reached an impasse
The third world war was in the air
What Robert was thinking when Lynn was walking with him
we do not know
Professor Stieglitz asserted his right to silence at the jury trial
Fräulein Werdenfels takes a photo of HERR MEISTER with flash
How many letters Robert had written to Edgar from London
we do not know
We suspect the catastrophe must have occurred
much earlier namely at the point
when Edgar relinquished his wealth
and returned to Switzerland to see his mother
Fräulein Werdenfels takes a photo of HERR MEISTER with flash
That lonely woman suffering from pneumonia
was waiting for Edgar in a hotel in Lausanne
which
by a strange coincidence
belonged to Professor Stieglitz
The brothers and sisters had come full circle
closes his manuscript
all applaud
PUBLISHER *in the middle of the applause*
That is great—
his head raised, turns to one side
just great

END

AFTERWORD

Thomas Bernhard (1931-1989), with Peter Handke the major figure in Austrian drama to emerge during the 1960s, grew up in deprived circumstances. Born illegitimate, he spent some time in a home for maladjusted children and dropped out of school at fifteen. At eighteen he contracted tuberculosis, which put an end to his hopes of a career as a singer. During his illness and convalescence he became interested in literature and began writing, mainly poetry. He also studied music and drama, graduating in 1957.

Bernhard first became more widely known as a writer of prose, his reputation being established with his first novel, *Frost*, published in 1963. In the 1970s he became one of the dominant writers for the German theater and also achieved international recognition. Despite their tone of provocation, their tirades against the cultural establishment, their attacks on Austria for its "collective amnesia" regarding the Nazi period, his plays were even commissioned by and performed at the usually ultra-conservative Salzburg Festival.

For many, his abuse of his own country was Bernhard's one and only theme, culminating in the scandal he provoked with his play *Heldenplatz* (Heroes' Square), written ostensibly to commemorate the centennial of the Vienna Burgtheater in 1988, a year which was also the fiftieth anniversary of the Nazi invasion of Austria and a time when Austria was going through the tribulations of the Waldheim affair. The virtuoso diatribes of the main character, an Austrian Jew returned from English exile, berating almost everything about modern-day Austria, but particularly its continuing anti-Semitism, set off a furore which, ironically, turned *Heldenplatz* into Bernhard's greatest success.

Just how awkward a person Bernhard was to have as one of the country's leading authors can be seen in a speech he gave at a ceremony when he was awarded a prize by the Ministry of Education and Culture, a speech which sent the minister walking out in high dudgeon: ". . . the times are imbecilic, the state is an organization that is condemned to repeated failure, the people to constant acts of infamy and mental deficiency." In his will he declared a ban on performances of his plays in Austria.

Although Bernhard's "befouling of his own nest" is the aspect of his works that hit the headlines, it is just the most obvious expression of what appears to be an all-encompassing pessimistic view of life. The figures he creates are almost all without exception morally and spiritually, often even physically deformed. The chronic illnesses many suffer from, or claim to suffer from, suggest that life itself is a disease which is only cured by death.

In particular Bernhard's plays pour scorn on the values the public holds dear, the values on which western civilization is founded. He reveals them to be empty gestures used to prop up the bloated self-esteem of his figures and often exploited to provide the physical comforts they claim to despise. Moritz Meister, the central figure of *Over All the Mountain Tops*, is a good example of this. Consequently, art and the humanities, as the public celebration of the values society is — or likes to think it is — based on, are often at the center of his works for the stage, though some plays, for example *Der Präsident* (The President) and *Vor dem Ruhestand* (Eve of Retirement) have a more directly political focus.

Bernhard's difficult early life may go some way to explaining his radical disenchantment with the world he lived in, the world, be it said, which provided his living. However, his presentation of life as absurd is so fundamental that it goes beyond explanation. His criticism is so absolute, it does not suggest the possibility of improvement; his negativism does not even imply a possible positive obverse, even a theoretical one.

This savage rejection of the modern world is reflected in a dramaturgy that is reduced to a minimum. Plot is almost nonexistent, repetition rather than development and conflict being the basic structural element in his plays. There is no exploration of the psychology of his characters, who often tend to be little more than the mouthpieces of their obsessions. Their common form of expression is the monologue, even when other characters are present. This can be seen at its clearest in the companion piece to *Over All the Mountain Tops, Der Weltverbesserer* (The World Fixer), in which the female partner of the central figure is mute for much of the play.

What saves Bernhard's plays from complete sterility, what the attraction is for the theatergoers who are also his victims — and seem mesmerized by his fireworks like a rabbit by the headlights of an oncoming car — is his linguistic virtuosity. Bernhard is a master of prose, his style often being described as "musical." Virtuosity of style should not here be confused with beauty. The way Bernhard lays out the language on the page, broken up into short lines of uneven length with no punctuation at all, makes it look as if it could be poetry. But it is a poetry which, as one commentator has put it, is "crippled": there is no regular metrical pattern, no rhyme nor even a rhythmical pulse. Its most conspicuous feature is repetition, yet it grips the audience with a — presumably horrified — fascination.

Over All the Mountain Tops (published 1981, first performed 1982) is Bernhard's satire on literature. The central figure, Moritz Meister, after years of disregard, has finally achieved the recognition he feels he richly deserves. He has adopted the pose of he "great writer," a national figure. He clearly sees himself as Germany's modern Goethe. Bernhard indicates this by the choice of name, *Meister*, meaning "master" or "maestro," is an obvious allusion to Wilhelm Meister, the hero of Goethe's novel. The title of the play is a quotation from a Goethe poem which, taken rather out of context, has for the German reader echoes of Goethe's reputation for Olympian aloofness. The Meisters' house, which they occupy rent-free from the town of his birth, stands high above the surrounding countryside. Another German high priest of literature, Thomas Mann, is also alluded to. There are hints of a self-portrait as well in, for example, Meister's poor origins and their contrast with his current splendid dwelling, his musicality and his weak chest.

That all this is a pose is made obvious in many ways. His high-sounding declarations contrast with the reality of his utter self-centeredness, his snobbery, his materialism, his love of comfort; his high-flown pronouncements on art, philosophy and life are empty, sometimes meaningless posturings; his great novel (whose main character is an obvious alter ego whom he quotes ad nauseam) is, from the passage he reads at the end of the play, dull and dreary and as superficial as Meister himself. The one poem of his that he quotes is incredibly trite.

But Meister is not the sole, perhaps not even the main target of Bernhard's scorn. The literary world takes him at his own estimation and fawns on him with embarrassing deference. The academic industry is represented by a doctoral student, the fortunate one among the many, allowed access because she is female, pretty and from a well-known upper-class family. The literary world is present in the person of a journalist from the arts section of the *Frankfurter Allgemeine Zeitung*, whose article on Meister will consist of fulsome flattery. Meister's publisher is full of fine phrases about culture and art, but his thinking is dominated by sales and profits.

Beyond these individuals, who anyway have a representative function, public bodies also come to worship at the master's shrine. Meister has just been elected a member of the Academy for Language and Literature and received a telegram of congratulation from the German President. Bernhard's satire reveals the whole of the public sphere of literature — and, by extension, of art and culture — to be a sham.

But, then, as the self-references in the character of Meister indicate, Bernhard and his play are part of that sphere. One is tempted to recall the plaintive cry of the man who writes to the author in Erich Kästner's poem, and asks, "But, Herr Bernhard, where's the positive side?" The reply, one suspects, would be the same: "Yes, devil only knows where that is."

Michael Mitchell